Contents

Android Essentials

Chris Haseman

So, you want to be an Android developer? Good, you've come to the right place. Whether you're a dabbler, professional, hobbyist, or coding junkie, I hope you've picked up my book out of a desire to learn about the somewhat schizophrenic world that is mobile development. Specifically, I hope you're interested in picking up the gauntlet thrown down by the Open Handset Alliance's Android team.

I took the opportunity to write this book because it's clear that Android has the potential to open up the mobile space in ways that keep us jaded mobile programmers up late at night. Volumes could be written about the errors of past platforms and the shortsightedness of an industry whose greatest achievement, at least here in America, is selling several million ringtones. You and your peers can bring about a long-needed change to the industry, perhaps bringing a much-needed breath of fresh air to an environment that, over the years, appears to have stagnated. You'll have to forgive my enthusiasm; it has been a long wait.

Chapter 1: Introduction

Before you start, we'll need to have a quick discussion about where you're beginning.

What You Need to Know to Start

It is a natural question you may be asking yourself: is this book for you? Yes, obviously, it is because you're reading it. However, I will make a few assumptions about your abilities:

- You understand Java; you can write it, read it, and grok it. Because this book is about the Android platform and not the language, I will be writing large amounts of Java code inline and assuming you can follow along. If your Java skills are rusty, I recommend checking out Apress's wealth of Java information on its site (`http://java.apress.com/`).

- Some familiarity with other mobile platforms will help you. As you move through the book, I'll make comparisons between Android and other mobile software development kits (SDKs). You don't need to be a professional mobile developer to follow along by any means.

- You have superior hacker skills. OK, not really, but if you're comfortable rolling up your proverbial sleeves and digging into the heart of a problem, you should feel right at home with this book.

- I will assume you have exactly zero experience developing for Android. If you've already mastered the basics, you may want to skip the first chapter and focus on the more advanced topics that follow.

That wasn't a big list, but it contained a few things that will help you follow the book with your sanity intact.

Ideally, I want this book to be useful and valuable to anyone interested in developing applications for Android. Hobbyists will find a foundation here for their dream application. Mobile game developers will find the nuts and bolts of graphical output and user input. Multimedia and application developers will find all the tricks, tips, and core functionality they need to put together the next major killer app. If you're a business-oriented person looking into porting your existing applications to Android, you'll find invaluable information on how to accomplish exactly that. In short, this book has a lot to offer you no matter your desired outcome, experience, time, or interest.

How to Best Use This Book

The simple answer is to read it, but this may mean different things to different people. If you're new to mobile development and Android, it would be best for you to treat this book as a tutorial. Follow along, chapter by chapter, until you have all the basics you need to get working.

If you're a more experienced Java and mobile programmer but are inexperienced with Android, you might want to treat this book as more of a reference manual after going through the first chapter to get a feel for things.

Throughout this work, I will primarily use real-world examples as a means to get you comfortable with Android. This book may not have a huge appeal to those who are already established veteran Android developers. As I said before, I will start from a place that assumes no prior experience with this SDK. This book will start simple: a splash screen, a main menu, and some simple multimedia. I'll then get into the more advanced concepts of Bluetooth, location-based services, background applications, and the other exciting features Android has to offer.

Enough talking, it's time to start.

Getting Started

It begins with installing the SDK. On a personal note, I'm doing all my development on Mac OS X with Eclipse. All screenshots, IDE information, tips, and tricks will be geared toward the Eclipse IDE. It seems the Android developers had the open source IDE Eclipse in mind, because they've released a plug-in that eases setup and debugging. For the sake of simplicity, I use Eclipse and the Open Handset Alliance's Android. I do not endorse this setup over any other. I will, however, take a little bit of time to walk through downloading and configuring Eclipse to integrate it with Android. If you're already up and running on the SDK, skip to "The Android Project" section. Additionally, you can find a much more in-depth install guide on Google's SDK installation page (`http://code.google.com/android/intro/installing.html#installingplugin`).

Installing Eclipse

Again, because Eclipse will be used in the book's examples, download the full version at `http://www.eclipse.org/downloads/`.

Be sure to get the Java EE version. It includes frameworks for a few editors that the full Google Eclipse plug-in will use. Install Eclipse; the default configurations should work just fine.

Note   With Windows and with the Mac, it's a good idea to keep your files and SDK installation out of folders that contain spaces. Many tools such as Ant, among others, can be confused by spaces in folder names.

Getting the Android SDK

You can find the Android SDK on Google's website at `http://code.google.com/android/download.html`.

Grab it, download it somewhere handy, and then unpack it. I've put mine in my `Development` folder at `/Developer/AndroidSDK`.

You can just as easily put the ZIP file anywhere on your filesystem. Just remember where you've stashed it, because you'll need to tell Eclipse where it is later. It's also a good idea, if you're a Windows or Linux user, to add the location of the Android tools to your Path variable.

Installing the Eclipse Plug-In

I like graphical user interfaces (GUIs), provided they have hotkeys like the Eclipse IDE, when working with Android. To get more than basic functionally out of the process, you'll need to download the Android Developer Tools. To install it from within Eclipse, follow the directions outlined by Google at `http://code.google.com/android/intro/`

`installing.html#installingplugin.`

If you've already installed the older version of the SDK and the Eclipse plug-in, I recommend you go back and update it to M5-RC15 (or the latest version) now using the previously mentioned links. Enough has changed between the older version and the latest that the changing details could be confusing. If you correctly follow the directions but get an error when trying to install the Android editors, go back and install the full version of Java EE Eclipse. The basic Java SDK doesn't include all the correct packages used by the Android plug-in.

Don't forget to point the Android plug-in to where you unpacked your copy of the SDK. It'll be in `Windows/Preferences/Android` on the Android tab.

Create a new project by selecting File ➤ New ➤ Android Project. Give the project and activity a pithy name of your choosing. You'll also have to insert into your source package name at least one dot (.), such as `apress.book.sample` or `crazy.flyingmonkey.application`.

Eclipse gives a fairly unhelpful error message if you forget to give it more than one name separated by dots. I can personally testify that this can be fairly frustrating if your brain is fried and you're, say, trying to get a book done on a deadline.

The Android Project

So, you're now the proud owner of your own basic Android application. If this isn't the case, because you skipped the previous section, create a new project right now. New projects, by default, have an implementation of "Hello, World." Books and articles that start by explaining "Hello, World" aren't particularly useful in my humble opinion. Consequently, I'm not going to take your time breaking down the functionality of the most basic Android application. What is worth taking some time to look into, however, are the contents, layout, and files of your new project. Let me briefly explain how each file and directory contributes to a functioning Android project (see Table 1-1).

Table 1-1. Files in a Basic Android Project

FILE NAME	PURPOSE
YourActivity.java	File for your default launch activity; more on this to follow.
R.java	File containing an ID for all asset constants.
Android Library/	Folder containing all Android's SDK files.
assets/	Multimedia and other miscellaneous required files.
res/	Base directory for resources used by the UI.
res/drawable	Directory for image files to be rendered by the UI layer.
res/layout	All XML-style view layout files are stored here. Again, more on this later.

Continued

Table 1-1. continued

FILE NAME	PURPOSE
res/values	Location for string's and configuration files.
AndroidManifest.xml	File that describes your application to the outside operating system.

Obviously, you've moved well beyond the days of Hello_World.c. As you move forward, I'll mention these files in passing. If you have trouble following later in the book, refer to this table. I'll take a few minutes to break down a few essentials.

Most central, and probably most confusing, among the various files is the Android manifest. This is the link between your application and the outside world. In this file, you will register intents for activities. (I'll get into intents and activities, as well as how they work, in the following chapter.) So that you have the groundwork for further development, Code Listing 1-1 shows what the Android manifest looks like when you create your first project.

Code Listing 1-1. Android Manifest.xml

```xml
<?xml version="1.0" encoding="utf-8"?>
<manifest xmlns:android="http://schemas.android.com/
    apk/res/android"package="apress.book.sample">
<application android:icon="@drawable/icon">
<activity android:name=".SampleApp"
    android:label="@string/app_name">
<intent-filter>
<action android:name="android.intent.action.MAIN" />
<category android:name=
    "android.intent.category.LAUNCHER" />
</intent-filter>
</activity>
</application>
</manifest>
```

After the `xml/declaration` comes the `<manifest>` tag with the schema URL. One of its properties is the name of your source package. In the case of this example, it is `apress.book.sample`.

Next up is the application declaration and location of the application icon. The `@drawable` notation indicates that the item can be found in the `res/drawable` folder. The application, at this point, consists of a single activity: `SampleApp`. The activity name is hard-coded, but its label, or what is displayed to the user within the Android application menu, is defined in the `res/values/strings.xml` file. The `@string` notation pulls the value from `app_name` within the aforementioned XML file.

Now you come to the intent filter. I will go into intent filters at length in the next chapter, but for now, you need to know that `android.intent.action.MAIN` and `android.intent.category.LAUNCHER` are predefined strings that tell Android which activity to fire up as your application is started.

That's all there is to the manifest file in its most basic form. For space reasons, I will try to avoid writing out the entire manifest file again. If you need context for elements that are being inserted later, dog-ear this page and return to it later.

Note   Get in the habit of moving as many strings, resources, and screen layouts into the `res` folder as much as humanly possible. It may cost you a little more time to work from these files up front, but once you start porting your application to the different languages, screen sizes, and function sets, your prep time will be paid back with interest. I'm sure this is something you read in computer manuals constantly, but it bears repeating. A little bit of planning and overhead up front can save you weeks of porting and debugging on the back side of a project. This is particularly important when developing for mobile devices, because each application can have many separate build environments.

Next up on the important file list is `R.java`. This file is where reference identification numbers live for all your resources, both graphical and drawable. Adding a new graphic to `res/drawable` should result in a corresponding identifier in the `R.java` class. References can then be made to these IDs rather than the items on the filesystem. This allows you to swap out strings for localization, screen size, and other errata that are guaranteed to change between devices.

You'll get into the other files as you add functionality to your repertoire. Let's get your application up and running.

Running, Debugging, and Causing General Mayhem

Running and debugging are, thankfully, extremely straightforward with Android. From within Eclipse, pull down the Run menu and select…wait for it…Run. This launches the Android emulator.

Tip   Once you've started the emulator for the first time, you don't need to quit or close it down. The latest version of the SDK ships with an emulator that can take minutes to "boot up." While the emulator is running, each subsequent Run or Debug execution will build and deploy your latest code to the emulator. The emulator will accept the changes and automatically launch your new project. This is the opposite of BREW or J2ME, which must relaunch after each change in your source base.

Once the Android emulator is up and running, you should see the "Hello World, *YourApplicationName*" message.

Again, "Hello, World" as a programming example is, for lack of a better term, emphatically lame, so I'll skip it and move on to a more practical example: a simple splash screen. Along the way, you should come to understand activities, intents, intent filters, services, and content providers.

Chapter 2: The Application

An application in Android is defined by the contents of its manifest. Each Android application declares all its activities, entry points, communication layers, permissions, and intents through `AndroidManifest.xml`. Four basic building blocks, when combined, comprise a rich Android application:

- *Activity*: The most basic building block of an Android application
- *Intent receiver*: A reactive object launched to handle a specific task
- *Service*: A background process with no user interface
- *Content provider*: A basic superclass framework for handling and storing data

In this chapter, I'll break down each specific piece with a concrete functional example. First up is the activity, the core building block of a stand-alone Android application.

Getting Active

All Android mobile applications, at least in the traditional sense, will revolve around an activity. If you've had any experience with other mobile platforms, Android's activity is quite similar to BREW's applet or Java ME's midlet. There are, however, a few very important differences.

Android vs. Java ME vs. BREW

A BREW application will, in the vast majority of all cases, consist of a single applet. That applet communicates with the rest of the handset through receiving and sending events. You can think of a Java ME application, on the other hand, as an extension of the `Midlet` class. The midlet has functions for starting, stopping, pausing, key handling, and performing any other interaction between the handset and application. A Java ME application usually consists of a single midlet.

Android applications can have any number of activities registered with the handset through the `AndroidManifest.xml` file. Android's multiactivity architecture is probably the major difference between developing for Android and developing for other handset SDKs. This single fact makes it much easier to write modular, compartmentalized code. In BREW and Java ME, a developer will implement most functionality within the confines of the midlet or the applet. In Android, you can write an activity, content handler, intent receiver, or service to handle nearly anything. Once you've written an activity to edit a text file, you can refer to this activity in all future applications you write by sending and receiving intent actions. This isn't to say that such architecture isn't possible within BREW or Java ME. It just has to be done at the Java, C, or C++ level or, in Brew, with cumbersome extensions instead of being built smoothly into the application framework.

Functionality

Just like the midlet, an activity uses a series of functions to interact with the outside world. At its base, your activity must override the method `onCreate`. Other functions you'll want to override are `onStop`, `onPause`, `onResume`, and `onKeyDown`. These few functions are what will let you tie your activity into the Android handset at large.

By default, new Android applications created within Eclipse will implement a "Hello, World" application. I'll show you how to go from this basic application to a fully functional splash screen.

Getting Splashy

You can download the packaged version of this splash screen example from the downloads section of `www.apress.com` if you want to use it as a starting point for your own Android application or you want to follow along in a more passive fashion. In this example, because it is your first, I will go through it in a series of small steps. I'll break down exactly what needs to be written, from adding a new image resource to modifying XML layout files. Down the road, examples will not parse out into such minute detail. This should be the only chapter that will read like a tutorial for beginners.

Adding the Image Resource

First you'll need a sample splash screen image. The "socially awkward" splash screen I've included is not going to win any awards, but it is a good poke at the rash of social networking applications that seem to keep cropping up in the mobile space right now.

To add this new resource, I've placed `menu_background.jpg` inside `res/drawable`. Make sure a new ID is added to `R.java`. It should look something like this:

```
public static final int menu_background=0x7f020001;
```

This is now your means of loading and drawing the image from within your code. You'll return to this concept in the next chapter on user interaction.

Creating an XML Layout File

Now that you have an image resource, you can add it to your XML layout file. These files are kept in `res/layout/`, and you should currently have one called `main.xml`. Add a new XML file called `splash.xml`, and copy the contents of the `main.xml` file into it. Next, modify the file by removing the `<TextView>` tag and add an `<ImageView>` tag that looks like the following:

```
<ImageView android:src="@drawable/menu_background"
android:layout_width="fill_parent"
    android:layout_height="fill_parent">
</ImageView>
```

Using Android's XML layout objects is simple and straightforward. As I mentioned, files in the `/res` directories can be referenced with the @

symbol as shown earlier, for example,
`android:src="@drawable/menu_background"`. Further, `layout_width`
and `layout_height` dictate the size of the image view. Look to make sure
your new layout file has been added to `R.java`. It should appear as
follows:

```
public static final int splash=0x7f030001;
```

Drawing the Splash Screen

Now that your splash screen is defined, it's time to activate and paint it.
Your existing Android activity is already drawing `main.xml`, so you'll
shift to your new splash layout. To make the switch, change this code:

```
setContentView(R.layout.main);
```

in the method `onCreate` to this code:

```
setContentView(R.layout.splash);
```

Run the application, and watch your newly created splash screen come to
life. If you've gotten errors thus far, check to make sure your names for
everything match up. If the image isn't drawing, make sure it's been
correctly placed in the `res/drawable` folder and that `splash.xml` refers
to the correct name and file.

Timing Is Almost Everything

The splash screen is now rendering, but splash screens alone make for
boring applications, so you'll need to move on to the main menu. You'll
use a simple inline-defined thread to accomplish the timing. There are a
few constants initialized before the thread that I've included. For the sake
of completeness, I've included the entirety of the `onCreate` method. Code
Listing 2-1 shows what mine looks like with the timing thread in place.

Code Listing 2-1. Timing the Splash Screen

```
long m_dwSplashTime = 3000;
boolean m_bPaused = false;
```

```java
boolean m_bSplashActive = true;

public void onCreate(Bundle icicle)
    {
super.onCreate(icicle);

        //Draw the splash screen
setContentView(R.layout.splash);
        //Very simple timer thread
        Thread splashTimer = new Thread()
        {
    public void run()
    {
        try
        {
            //Wait loop
            long ms = 0;
            while(m_bSplashActive && ms < m_dwSplashTime)
            {
                sleep(100);
                //Advance the timer only if we're running.
                if(!m_bPaused)
                    ms += 100;
            }
            //Advance to the next screen.
            startActivity(new Intent(
                "com.google.app.splashy.CLEARSPLASH"));
        }
        catch(Exception e)
{
    Log.e("Splash", e.toString());
}
        finally
        {
            finish();
        }
    }
        };
        splashTimer.start();
}
```

At long last, you're getting into some Java code. This simple thread will run until the time counter exceeds `m_dwSplashTime`. Although there are other methods for implementing a timer, I like this one for two reasons:

- It can be paused. The timer will advance only if the `m_bPaused` flag is `false`. As you'll see in a minute, it's easy to suspend the timer if your activity's `onPause` method is called. This is not always a requirement for a splash screen, but it is important for other timing-based operations.

- Moving to the next screen is as simple as flipping the `m_bSplashActive` flag to `false`. Advancing to the next screen, if you implement it in this fashion, does not require you to make the move and then cancel a more traditional timer.

With this code in place, you should see the splash screen for as long as you set `m_dwSplashTime` in milliseconds. When that time is up or the user interrupts the splash screen with a key press, `startActivity` will be called (I'll explain this shortly). This function will move the user to what will become the main menu in the next chapter. `finish` closes down the splash activity so the user does not return to it when they press Back from the main menu. You'll need to implement an activity that accepts the `CLEARSPLASH` intent action. In the meantime, let's review a few other important activity methods you'll want to override.

Pause, Resume, Rinse, Repeat

Pausing the splash timer when your activity is suspended by an incoming call, SMS message, or other interruption is as easy as the following:

```
protected void onPause()
{
    super.onPause();
    m_bPaused = true;
}
```

As with most of these overridden methods, you'll need to invoke the superclass before doing anything else. If you review the timer thread, you'll see that the ms counter responsible for keeping track of time passed doesn't advance if m_bPaused is true. At this point, I'm sure you can guess what onResume will look like:

```
protected void onResume()
{
    super.onResume();
    m_bPaused = false;
}
```

No surprises here. When your application is resumed, the timer thread will resume adding time to the ms counter.

Basic Key Handling

Key handling within the activity is handled by overriding the onKeyDown method. We'll use this function to allow a user to cancel your fledgling splash screen. As you can see in the timer thread at the start of this section, you've set up an escape clause in the timer loop by the name of m_bSplashActive. To escape, you'll just override the onKeyDown method so that it flips the splash flag to false. Here's the code you'll need to add:

```
public boolean onKeyDown(int keyCode, KeyEvent event)
{
    //if we get any key, clear the splash screen
    super.onKeyDown(keyCode, event);
    m_bSplashActive = false;
    return true;
}
```

Now, when the user hits any key, the screen will be advanced on the next trip through the timer loop.

Clear Intent

There's one more thing you'll need to do before you're done with the splash screen. I'm sure you're wondering about that `startActivity` method call earlier. This means it's time to talk briefly, in this limited context, about the intent. An *intent* is an object that functions as a communication event between two or more activities, content handlers, intent receivers, or services. In this case, you will call `startActivity` with the intent `com.google.app.splashy.CLEARSPLASH`. When `startActivity` is called, Android searches all its manifests for the node that has registered for the aforementioned `CLEARSPLASH` intent action. It just so happens that you'll add your own activity called `MainMenu` that will register for just such an intent.

To create what will become the main menu activity, add a new class to your existing source package called `MainMenu`. Next, make sure it extends the `Activity` class, implements `onCreate`, and calls `setContentView` on `R.layout.main`. At this point, you'll want to open `AndroidManifest.xml` and add a new activity element to it. After the

`</activity>` closing tag of the splash screen, you should insert the following:

```
<activity android:name=".MainMenu"
        android:label="@string/app_name">
    <intent-filter>
        <action android:name=
           "com.google.app.splashy.CLEARSPLASH"/>
  <category android:name=
           "android.intent.category.DEFAULT"/>
    </intent-filter>
</activity>
```

Define the activity's name as `.MainMenu`. This will tell Android which Java class to load and run. Register, within the intent filter tag, for the `com.apress.splash.CLEARSPLASH` intent action. In reality, the name of the intent could be `beef.funkporium.swizzle`, and as long as the name is consistent between the `startActivity` call and the snippet of the Android manifest listed earlier, all the right things should continue to happen.

Running It

Running your application at this point should result, if you've paid attention thus far, in your splash screen being drawn for a few seconds, followed by your new main menu activity taking focus. It should also be impossible to get back to the splash screen once your application has advanced to the main menu. If you're having trouble, make sure your new main menu is listed in the manifest and in `R.java`. Also, make sure you're drawing the correct layout file within your new intent.

The Life Cycle of an Activity

The life cycle of an activity is covered extensively in the Google documentation. However, if I'm reviewing the nuts and bolts of what makes an activity, I cannot pass by this important information. At this point, with your splash screen, you should be ready to roll.

For explanation's sake, I've also added the following functions to the splash screen activity:

```
protected void onStop()
{
    super.onStop();
}
protected void onDestroy()
{
    super.onDestroy();
}
```

If you place breakpoints in all the functions within your new splash activity and run it in debug mode, you'll see the breakpoints hit in the following order:

1. `onCreate`

2. `onStart`

3. `onResume`

4. At this point, your activity is now running. Three seconds in, the timer thread will reach its end and call `startActivity` with the splash clearing intent. Next, it will call `finish`, which tells Android to shut down the splash screen activity.

5. `onPause`

6. `onStop`

7. `onDestroy`

This is the general life cycle of an activity from start to finish. You can find a much more comprehensive exposé on the life and times of an Android activity in Google's documentation at `http://code.google.com/android/reference/android/app/Activity.html`. You'll even find a spiffy graph. In essence, the handset uses a combination of the previous functions to alert you to the major events that can occur in your application: starting, closing, suspending, and resuming. Activities, as I've covered before, are going to be the core building block of any traditional application; they give you control over the screen and the ability to receive user inputs. You'll get more into user interaction in later chapters.

Thus Far

So far I've explored how activities are integrated within the phone, how they are started and stopped, and how they communicate on a basic level. I've demonstrated how to display a simple XML view screen and how to switch between two actives both in reaction to a key event and at the end of a set amount of time. In the short-term, you'll need to learn more about how Android uses intents, intent receivers, and intent filters to communicate. To do this, you'll need another sample application.

Creating the Intent Receiver

An *intent receiver* is one of the few things in Android that does exactly what its name implies. Its role is to hang around waiting for registered intent actions, Android's version of BREW-style notifications. I'll use a somewhat less production-worthy application to demonstrate one of the trickier tasks of an intent receiver: receiving and reacting to incoming text messages.

Setting It Up

Let me paint you a picture. You've returned to your desk one afternoon to discover that you've fallen victim to a Hello Kitty attack. Your office desk is covered, from carpet to ceiling, with cute pink images of the most annoying icon known to humankind. You know who's done it, and it's payback time. You also know that your VP of engineering hates a particular song with a fiery passion matched by nothing else. That song is "La Bamba." You decide to get even by rigging your co-worker's Android phone with a sleeper application. I'll show you how to make an Android application that will respond to a specific SMS message by playing an audio file for maximum humiliation effect. This will make your newfound enemy the subject of intense anger from your VP. At the same time, you'll want your victim to know he's been had…and give him a chance to shut the sound off. This prank application requires an intent receiver, an activity, a service, and the means for all three to communicate. Imagine your co-worker's surprise when his phone starts spouting the very song your VP of engineering hates most in the world.

What Practical Use Could This Possibly Have?

This is an excellent question. Although on the surface this may not seem to be the most practical of applications, I'm sure, with a little imagination, you can come up with a variety of important realistic uses for this little prank application, from push e-mail notifications to interphone application communication. Besides, things have been far too serious thus far.

You'll move forward in four stages. In each phase, you'll learn more about intent receivers, services, and the interactions between all these application pieces:

- Being notified on arrival of an SMS

- Opening the contents of an SMS and looking for a specific payload

- Starting an activity when the SMS arrives and being aware that the startup has occurred at the behest of the intent receiver

- Starting a new service that will play an audio file

Using Intent Receivers

Before you get into building the intent receiver, you need to take a quick moment to learn why you would use one. Intent receivers have little to no memory footprint, linkage, or overhead. Where an activity has to load all of its heavy imported classes on startup, an intent receiver has none of these obligations. Because new intents of a certain type could arrive with crushing frequency (network status updates, for example), a lightweight object must take the first pass at parsing the data. If it is an appropriate time to awaken a larger UI process or hefty background service, the intent receiver should take such an action.

Tip   Intent receivers can be started and closed frequently (depending on what they listen for); try to make them lightweight and use as few libraries as you can get away with. Your users will not be happy if their phone is slowed to a crawl because you've inserted too much overhead into the processing of any particular event.

Building the Intent Receiver

First things first—you'll need to create a new project for the little prank application. In the source directory, create a new class that will become the new intent receiver. At first pass, it should look like this:

```
public class PrankSMSReceiver extends IntentReceiver
{
    public void onReceiveIntent
                (Context context, Intent intent)
    {
        return;
    }
}
```

Now that you have the class set up, you'll need to tell Android you'd like to receive SMS events. You do this by modifying the `AndroidManifest.xml` file to give you permission and to register for the `RECEIVE_SMS` intent action.

Permissions

Carriers, users, and even developers may not want to give Android applications free reign to run through the privileged layers of their handsets and networks. Consequently, Google has introduced a notion of permissions in Android (something all developers with previous mobile experience should recognize). To be able to receive SMS messages, you'll need to notify the handset that you're allowed to receive them.

Because permissions, in Android, are declared for all elements within a particular manifest, you'll add the permissions line after the `<manifest>` declaration tag (Code Listing 2-2). The sample app will be called `PrankApp`. Its main activity is called `PrankActivity`. No namespace prizes should be given to this writer for originality.

Code Listing 2-2. Adding Permissions to Receive SMS Messages

```
<?xml version="1.0" encoding="utf-8"?>
<manifest xmlns:android=
    "http://schemas.android.com/apk/res/android"
    package="com.apress.book.PrankApp">
    <uses-permission android:name=
        "android.permission.RECEIVE_SMS" />
```

Without the permissions flag, Android will not launch your application when it receives an SMS. There are other permissions I'll need to cover as you move along. In the meantime, you can find a list of all permissions in Android's documentation at `http://code.google.com/android/reference/android/Manifest.permission.html`.

Send Me SMS Too!

Now that you have permission to interact with the SMS layer of the handset, you have to tell the handset what to do when a new text message arrives. To accomplish this, you must open the `AndroidManifest.xml` file as you've done before. You'll add a new intent receiver alongside the existing activity. Code Listing 2-3 shows what to insert (I've left the `</activity>` tag in place for reference).

Code Listing 2-3. Registering the New Intent Receiver for Incoming SMSs

```
</activity>
<receiver android:name=
        "PrankSMSReceiver"android:enabled="true">
    <intent-filter>

<actionandroid:name="android.provider.Telephony.SMS_RECEIVED"
/>

<categoryandroid:name="android.intent.category.DEFAULT" />
    </intent-filter>
</receiver>
```

That's all you should need to receive an intent notification each time the handset gets an incoming SMS.

Seeing the Intent Receiver in Action

This is a little more difficult to pull off than it sounds. A process must be running for the DDMS (the debugger application) to attach to it. But in most cases you don't want the application to run except when a new event triggers it. The solution is a little bit of a shell game with the Eclipse IDE. This may get a little more complicated as you advance to the later steps.

Place a breakpoint inside your `onReceiveIntent` method. Start debugging the application, and let the emulator sit on the "Hello World, PrankActivity" screen.

In Eclipse, switch views to the DDMS. You can do this by pressing Command+F8 a few times or by selecting the menu Window ➤ Open Perspective ➤ DDMS.

Figure 2-1 shows what it looks like.

Figure 2-1. The DDMS perspective

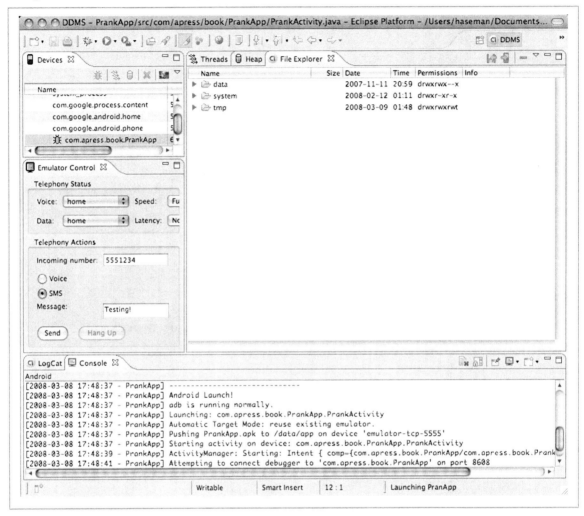

Along the left window, on the Devices tab, you should now see your application highlighted with a little green bug next to it. This is the DDMS telling you that the debugger is attached to your `PrankApp` process. A little further down is Emulator Control tab. This is where you'll send the SMS message. Enter any phone number first, select SMS, type a test message, and hit Send.

You should, if you've set up your manifest correctly, see Eclipse switch back to the Debug perspective and halt on your newly set breakpoint.

Note   If nothing is happening, first make sure you've set the permissions correctly. If they're not correct, you should see a failed permissions message go by on the bottom of the DDMS screen on the LogCat tab. Also, make sure your application is already running and has the green debugging icon next to it on the Devices tab. If all else fails, compare your project with the sample one I've included with this book.

If you've correctly followed along so far, your intent's `onReceiveIntent` function will now be called each time an SMS message is sent to the handset. Next, you'll have to figure out how to retrieve the contents of an SMS message.

What's in an SMS?

Sadly, to date, Android's documentation on receiving and filtering SMS messages is confusing at best. I suspect it's not a feature that's high on the list of things to tell developers about. Although I disagree with these priorities, it gives me a chance to fill the gap.

Here's what the `methodonReceiveIntent` looks like now that you're listening for new SMS messages:

```
public void onReceiveIntent
      (Context context, Intent intent)
{
  SmsMessage msg[] =
  Telephony.Sms.Intents.getMessagesFromIntent(intent);
    for(int i = 0; i < msg.length; i++)
      {
          String msgTxt = msg[i].getMessageBody();
          if (msgTxt.equals("0xBADCAT0_Fire_The_Missiles!"))
          {
```

```
            //Start the pranking here
        }
    }

    return;
}
```

You'll also need to import two libraries to make this work:

```
import android.telephony.gsm.SmsMessage;
import android.provider.Telephony;
```

Buried in the Telephony library is the call `getMessageFromIntent`, which will return an array of SMS messages. All that's left is pulling the payload out of the SMS messages in question. The special code you'll be looking for to trigger your prank activity is the text "0xBADCAT0_Fire_The_Missiles!"

It must be a combination suitably unique so that it will not be triggered by accident. You wouldn't want your prank to misfire and alert the victim too early.

Note   In Android, features that are not documented well are very likely not finished. Because the documentation for receiving SMS messages is nearly nonexistent, you should expect some changes in how SMSs are processed. More than likely, the overall method should be similar, but it's safe to assume that some of the details will change before the SDK reaches its final version. This example is more about learning how to use an intent receiver than it is about the particulars of text message communication.

Triggering the Activity

It's important to remember that the life cycle of an intent receiver lasts only as long as the method call `onReceiveIntent`. Once out of that function, Android is free to kill the process running your application. Any asynchronous functionality will die a messy death if started. If you want to do anything beyond simple processing within the method, you'll need to start a service or an activity. Since you want to both play music and alert your victim that they've been had, you'll need to start up an activity. You accomplish this as follows:

```
if (msgTxt.equals("0xBADCAT0_Fire_The_Missiles!"))
{
//Start the Activity
    Intent startActivity = new Intent();
    startActivity.setLaunchFlags(Intent.NEW_TASK_LAUNCH);
    startActivity.setAction("com.apress.START_THE_MUSIC");
    context.startActivity(startActivity);
}
```

The only unrecognizable code you'll see here is the addition of NEW_TASK_LAUNCH in setLaunchFlags. You'll need to do this any time you want to send out an intent action that will start a new activity. Additionally, just as you did in the splash screen example application, you'll have to add a new action to the intent filter of your activity. The process should look familiar:

```
<intent-filter>
<action android:name="android.intent.action.MAIN" />
<action android:name="com.apress.START_THE_MUSIC" />
<category android:name=
    "android.intent.category.LAUNCHER" />
<category android:name=
    "android.intent.category.DEFAULT" />
</intent-filter>
```

Now, if you've correctly added the earlier code in place, when you send a SMS message from the DDMS perspective, you should see your application come to the foreground and the "Hello World, PrankActivity" text display proudly on the screen.

Rigging the Activity

There is one last piece you'll need to add before getting into the more dastardly music playback service: rigging up the activity to correctly respond to the action sent by your SMS intent receiver. If the application is started normally, you'll want to immediately close it down. Again, you can't have the victim of your prank launching it from the menus and clueing in to your plan too early. To do this, you'll have to retrieve the launching intent and call the `getAction` method to figure out under what case it has been launched. The `PrankActivity`'s `onCreate` method should now look like Code Listing 2-4.

Code Listing 2-4. Launching on a Specific Intent Action

```
public void onCreate(Bundle icicle)
{
super.onCreate(icicle);

    Intent i = getIntent();
    String action = i.getAction();
    if (action != null &&
     action.equals("com.apress.START_THE_MUSIC"))
    {
        setContentView(R.layout.pranked);
        //We'll need to start the music service here
    }
    else
        finish();
}
```

First you'll get the intent that launched your activity. With the intent in hand, you can retrieve the calling action with the `getAction` method. This will return a string containing the launching event that you'll check against your known music action listed in the previous XML. If the launch event for your activity comes from normal means (from the menu or from starting the debugger), the action string will be null. If this is the case, you'll want to shut down the activity immediately using the `finish` method.

Note   The `onCreate` method is called only when your application is started for the first time. If you've launched your application and then exited it (using the Back key), the application will still be running in the background. If, at that point, you send the SMS message, your activity will come back to the foreground, but its `onStart` method will be called but not `onCreate`. Feel free to move the functionality of your own sample (if you're following along) to the `onStart` method.

Who Do You Want to Humiliate Today?

Although it might be a little overkill, you'll use one of Android's `Service` objects to handle music playback. I'm going to do it this way for two reasons:

- It's a great chance to demonstrate the use of a service in a simple, uncomplicated environment.

- Potentially, it will let you start up the music without a visible application presence, making your prank application that much more dastardly.

Nervous with the Service

Why would you want to use a service? Essentially, it's meant to be an object that runs as a separated process from the user interface. It's perfect for cases when a developer wants functionality (be it network or multimedia related) to be able to run independently. Examples include audio playback, background web transactions, and evil prank applications. Although services allow multiple applications to bind (to open a communications channel), with them you'll be using it as a simple background process. Again, services have a wealth of uses beyond the simple one you're putting them to here.

Creating a Service

Add a new class to your source package. I've called my `PrankService` again (no points for originality). At its most basic level, a service must override the `onBind` method. To get a service class to compile, it must look, at least a little bit, like Code Listing 2-5.

Code Listing 2-5. A Stripped-Down Service

```
public class PrankService extends Service
{
    public IBinder onBind(Intent intent)
    {
        return null;
    }
}
```

For this example, you won't be using the `onBind` method of the service interaction. You'll simply be starting and stopping the service from within your main activity. To do this, you'll have to override two more methods within the `Service` class:

- `onStart(int startId, Bundle arguments)`
- `onDestroy()`

When `onStart` is called, you'll begin playing your sample media file. When the service is destroyed, you'll explicitly stop it. This is not necessarily required, but you'll spell it out a little more later for the sake of explanation.

Starting the Service

Starting a new service should look similar to starting an activity. Since you've already been exposed to this a few times before, I'll just drop in the code and let you sort it out yourself.

Recall the `onCreate` method within `PrankActivity` listed earlier. Simply replace the comment "We'll need to start the music service here" with the following line of code:

```
startService(new Intent
    ("com.apress.START_AUDIO_SERVICE"), null);
```

Again, this should look familiar. The only difference between starting an activity and starting a service (aside from the different method call) is the ability to pass a *bundle* (essentially a map or hash table) of parameters along with the intent. That bundle will be passed to the `onCreate` method of the service.

Starting the Music

Like BREW and Java ME, Android has made media playback (at least on a simple play/stop basis) very simple and easy to use. When your service's `onStart` function is called, you'll load and play a test audio file from the `/res/raw` directory. The first order of business is to copy a sample audio file into `/res/raw` (if you don't have this directory, go ahead and create it). Next, drop your humiliating, and copy-write respecting, audio file into the `raw` folder. If you're using Eclipse, you should add a corresponding element to `R.raw`. In your case, it's `R.raw.test`.

Now that you have a music file to reference, you can add the procedural calls to your `PrankService` as follows:

```
public void onStart(int startId, Bundle arguments)
{
    MediaPlayer p;
    super.onStart(startId, arguments);
    player = MediaPlayer.create(this, R.raw.test);
    player.start();
}
```

Remember, `onStart` is an overridden method, so you'll have to call the superclass version of the same function first, or Android will get cranky with you. At that point, you'll just have the `MediaPlayer` static class create a new media player object. Because a service is a child of the `Context` class, you'll pass a pointer to your current context and the static variable representing your test media. At this point, you can call `play`, and you're off to the races. Playback should continue in the background with this service until the `stopService` method is called by your main activity. When `stopService` is called, the following method will be called:

```
public void onDestroy()
{
    super.onDestroy();
    player.stop();
}
```

An Act of Mercy

Since you're being a nice prankster, you'll give your victim a way out. As you've seen before, the activity is triggered by the intent receiver at which point the activity starts the service. As you've just seen, the service is responsible for playing the noise that will so irritate your fictional VP of engineering. Again, because you're being merciful in your execution of payback, you'll have to build in a way for the victim to turn off the music. Adding the following method in your `PrankActivity` can accomplish your act of grace:

```
public boolean onKeyDown(int keyCode, KeyEvent event)
{
    stopService(new Intent(
            "com.apress.START_AUDIO_SERVICE"));
    finish();
    return true;
}
```

Manifestation

Here's what the manifestation looks like:

```
<service android:name=".PrankService">
    <intent-filter>
```

```
      <action android:name=
        "com.apress.START_AUDIO_SERVICE" />
      <category android:name=
        "android.intent.category.DEFAULT" />
    </intent-filter>
  </service>
```

Zen and the Art of Getting Even

Through the use of a devious little prank application, you've explored how
intents, intent receivers, services, and activities work together in an
advanced, mostly background, application. I'll now go over, step by step,
what you did and how you accomplished it.

Getting It Done

You did the following:

1. You used an intent receiver with the right permissions and a system-level
   SMS intent to arrange for your `PrankSMSReciever` object to be
   instantiated each time an SMS arrives on the phone. If your intent receiver
   detected a very specific SMS payload, it would respond by sending an
   intent that would start your activity.

2. This activity, named `PrankActivity`, would listen for the specific intent
   action sent by the `PrankSMSReceiver`. When it received that precise
   intent action, your activity would display a "gotcha" message to the
   victim. At the same time, the activity would send out an intent meant to
   start up a service. If, at any point the victim/user pressed a key on the
   phone, the application would exit, and the music service would be
   terminated.

3. The service class, called `PrankService`, listening for the
   `PrankActivity`'s intent, would start and begin to play an obnoxious,
   predefined audio file. It would continue to play until it was told to stop by
   the `PrankActivity`'s call to the method `stopService`.

Note   This sample application does not deal with the handset's native SMS application. Because all intent receivers are notified of an incoming intent, your application will be competing for user attention with Android's SMS inbox application. In production, this may require a substantial timer and perhaps a trigger text payload, which is a little more subtle than "0xBADCAT0_Fire_The_Missiles!"

FURTHER DEVIOUSNESS

Here are a few ways you can explore and extend the prank application on your own:

- Get more evil by taking the activity out of the loop. Launch the `PrankService` directly from the intent receiver. Do not give the victim a way of shutting off the music.

- Add a different text payload to stop the music. This exercise would be an excellent one to combine with the previous one.

- Customize your "get even" message. Create a prefix that triggers the service and a payload, which is displayed by the main app activity. Pass this payload from the intent receiver to the activity using a payload within the intent. Taunting, sometimes, needs fine-tuning.

These are just a few ways you can better learn the pieces of Android while at the same time making life miserable for those around you.

Moving Data in Android

Finally, to round your knowledge about Android's application building blocks, you need to focus on the content resolver. Android does not give the SDK particular access to the phones filesystem, as Brew does. Nor does it offer a `RecordStore`, as does Java ME. Your primary method for passing data between your activities, intent receivers, and services is going to be through the `ContentResolver` superclass. Though you can store data through files, preferences, and other databases, content resolvers can take many forms, and Android ships with a few important content resolvers built in. Here's a list, at time of publication, of the major Android content resolvers you'll probably want to interact with on a regular basis:

- Browser
  - Bookmarks
  - Search history
- Phone calls
  - Call log
  - Recent calls
- Contacts
- System settings
  - Hardware settings (Bluetooth, networking settings)
  - Software settings

Android's documentation gives an excellent walk-through of using the contacts content resolver here: `http://code.google.com/android/ devel/data/contentproviders.html#usingacp`.

Quickly, I'll walk you through adding a bookmark to the phone browser's bookmark list. First, you'll want to search the current list of bookmarks to see whether your link is in place. Second, you'll add your bookmark if it isn't there.

Note   It is possible to create your own content providers as a way to wrap Android's SQLite implementation for universal access. You'll get into how to do this in later chapters. For now you're just going to handle the "client" side of this content resolver interaction.

Android uses a custom implementation of SQLite to store information locally. If you're not familiar with the basics of SQL, now might be a good time to brush up. I'm going to assume, for the sake of expediency, that you understand basic SQL searching commands. If you need to brush up, Apress has an excellent resource at `http://apress.com/book/catalog?category=145`.

Shameless Self-Promotion

Let's say in the "About" section of your application that you want to have a button that adds your commercial software page to the user's web bookmarks. You want to make sure it isn't added twice if your user has clicked the button again by accident. For the sake of this simple demonstration, you'll trigger this event in your sample application when the user presses a key.

Note   On an amusing note, if you need proof, as a developer, that Android is still not quite fully baked, you need look no further than the documentation for `android.content.ContentResolver` under the method `getDataFilePath`, which states "DO NOT USE THIS FUNCTION!! Someone added this, and they shouldn't have. You do not have direct access to files inside of a content provider. Don't touch this. Go away." It's good to know that even the technical writers for Android's documentation have a sense of humor.

Fetching the User's Bookmarks

It should be obvious, at least at this point, that a developer could do some fairly nefarious things with access to a user's bookmarks. It's not clear, at this point, what Android will do to keep this sort of thing from happening. I suppose it's up to the carriers to lock down or monitor this behavior. In any case, you'll use a call to the method `managedQuery`, which will return a list of the user's bookmarks:

```
Cursor bookmarks =
    android.provider.Browser.getAllBookmarks
    (getContentResolver());
int urlColumn = bookmarks.getColumnIndex(
android.provider.Browser.BookmarkColumns.URL);
Cursor results;
String[] proj = new String[]
    {
        android.provider.BaseColumns._ID,
        android.provider.Browser.BookmarkColumns.URL,
        android.provider.Browser.BookmarkColumns.TITLE
    };
results =
    managedQuery(android.provider.Browser.BOOKMARKS_URI,
     proj, null,
    android.provider.Browser.BookmarkColumns.URL
    + " ASC");
```

I'll now break down what's happening. You'll first get the column index of the bookmark URL. Again, because Android provides access to most of its internal data in a SQL format, you should get used to referring to your saved information in a database-centric way. Next you'll set up the cursor, an object similar to a Java ME RecordStore enumerator and set up your projection string array. Because you're interested only in the columns containing the URL, you can keep it very simple. The method call managedQuery is the call that will return your data. You'll pass in the URI string for the bookmarks store, hand it your simple projection array, leave the where section empty, and tell it to sort the URLs in descending order.

Searching the Results

Searching through the results is as simple as iterating through the Curser object and pulling out a string from the URL column id you retrieved earlier:

```
Cursor results =
    android.provider.Browser.getAllBookmarks
    (getContentResolver());
int urlColumn =
```

```
results.getColumnIndex
    (android.provider.Browser.BookmarkColumns.URL);
results.first();
do
{
    //url is a method param
    //containing what we're looking for
    if(results.getString(urlColumn).equals(url))
        return false;
} while(results.next());
```

You could do more based on the contents of the URL, but for now you'll just look for your www.apress.com link. Obviously, if this code were run with the aforementioned Apress URL, you won't find it. Since the user wants to add your corporate URL in your fictional "About" section, you'll have to oblige them.

Adding Evil Corporate URLS with a Content Resolver

Maybe they aren't evil, but you'll add them anyway. Since Apress is probably one of the least evil of companies out there (not that I'm biased, mind you), you'll let them get away with it, just this once. Here's the fancy ContentReceiver way of adding the bookmark records:

```
ContentValues inputValues = new ContentValues();
inputValues.put
    (android.provider.Browser.BookmarkColumns.BOOKMARK,
    "1");
inputValues.put
    (android.provider.Browser.BookmarkColumns.URL,
    "http://www.apress.com/");
inputValues.put
    (android.provider.Browser.BookmarkColumns.TITLE,
      "Apress, the not so evil company");

ContentResolver cr = getContentResolver();
Uri uri =
cr.insert
    (android.provider.Browser.BOOKMARKS_URI,
      inputValues);
```

As with most SDKs, there's more than one way to accomplish the same task. Earlier, you had the more complex way of adding a bookmark. This approach is useful because it gives you a reference for how to add elements through a `ContentResolver` that doesn't have helper functions. Now, here's the easy way:

```
android.provider.Browser.saveBookmark(this, "Apress", url);
```

The helper function will activate a dialog box asking the user to confirm the bookmark add. This is probably the most user-friendly way of adding bookmarks—unless you want to control what the dialog box looks like.

Part of This Balanced Breakfast

In the past three examples you explored all of Android's major building blocks. You started by looking at a functional splash screen. This let you explore the essentials of starting, maintaining, and moving through the `Activity` object. It let you get your foot though the door about intents and interprocess/object communication. Using and passing intents between activities, services, content handlers, and intent receivers is probably one of the most important things that sets Android apart from the other mobile environments.

With activities and communication basics under your belt, you moved on to the service and intent receiver. To use these two building blocks, you cooked up a devious prank application that would both force you to use all three pieces (activity, service, and intent receiver) and make all three communicate with each other. Almost as a side note, you explored what it takes to be notified when an SMS message arrives on the phone.

Last, you explored how to retrieve and write to a content resolver that is native to the device: the browser's bookmark database. Proof that things do not always go as planned, Android rebuffed your attempts at adding a new bookmark through the traditional content resolver method, which forced you to fall back on a helper function designed to do the same thing. Now that I've covered the basics, it's time to let the handset user weigh in a little more.

Chapter 3: User Interface

In Soviet Google, the Interface Renders You

In the scrum of mobile UI development architectures, Android's rises to the top. If you have some mobile experience, you'll find it to be a happy union of Java ME's `Canvas/Screen` object and the BREW widget hierarchy, with some XML layout tools to boot. Each activity, as it's launched from within your application, is placed on a screen stack. Android is already configured to handle closing down the top activity and activating the one under it when you ask or when the user presses Back. This setup allows you to think of every activity as the base for a single screen.

Each activity may contain different views and view groups in a hierarchical tree. You can visualize this tree with the view groups and layout objects as the trunk and branches (because view group objects can be cast into views) and with the views or widgets as the leaves. A single *view*, in its most basic format, is a drawable rectangle. A *view group*, in its most basic format, is an object containing one or more views. This object hierarchy allows you to lay out complex user interfaces without having to go through the error-prone process of calculating view rectangles and widget overlap maps. If, on the other hand, that sort of thing is your bag, Android will stay out of the way and let you render in the style of Java ME's hand-drawn game canvas.

In this chapter, you'll start with basic XML-based screen layouts and move toward the more complex custom canvas drawing. For the sake of this book, I'll break down and discuss views as three major food groups:

- *XML-defined widgets/views and view groups*: Good for basic information display and menus

- *Android native views*: `TextViews`, `LayoutGroups`, `ScrollBars`, and text entry

- *Custom views*: The game programmer's best friend

You'll start with a sample login screen, move into manipulating and laying out widgets and views in code, and finally render an interactive animation with a custom view.

Easy and Fast, the XML Layout

Getting started with XML layouts might seem simple at first, but it's going to get complicated really quickly. You'll start with the layouts and work your way down to the individual elements.

Laying Out

Most XML screens will be wrapped in a layout object. Layout objects come in many different flavors, each of which you'll look at really quickly and then check out with a simple example in the following sections.

Caution   At compile time, these XML layout files are parsed and packed by Android into a tight binary format. This saves monstrous amounts of parsing time on startup. However, it means that the XML files cannot be changed by your code during runtime. More specifically, you may be able to change these XML files during execution, but it will do absolutely nothing to the layout of your application. Additionally, you have to pay a small performance price for inflating a view or view group from XML. Your mileage may vary depending on CPU load and UI complexity.

LinearLayout

All elements are arranged in a descending column from top to bottom or left to right. Each element can have gravity and weight properties that denote how they dynamically grow and shrink to fill space. Elements arrange themselves in a row or column notation based on the `android:orientation` parameter. For example (see Figure 3-1):

```
<LinearLayout xmlns:android=
    "http://schemas.android.com/apk/res/android"
    android:orientation="vertical"
    android:layout_width="fill_parent"
    android:layout_height="fill_parent"
>
<TextView
    android:layout_width="wrap_content"
    android:layout_height="wrap_content"
    android:text="Element One"
    />
<TextView
    android:layout_width="wrap_content"
    android:layout_height="wrap_content"
    android:text="Element Two"
    />
<TextView
    android:layout_width="wrap_content"
    android:layout_height="wrap_content"
    android:text="Element Three"
    />
</LinearLayout>
```

Figure 3-1. Linear layout example

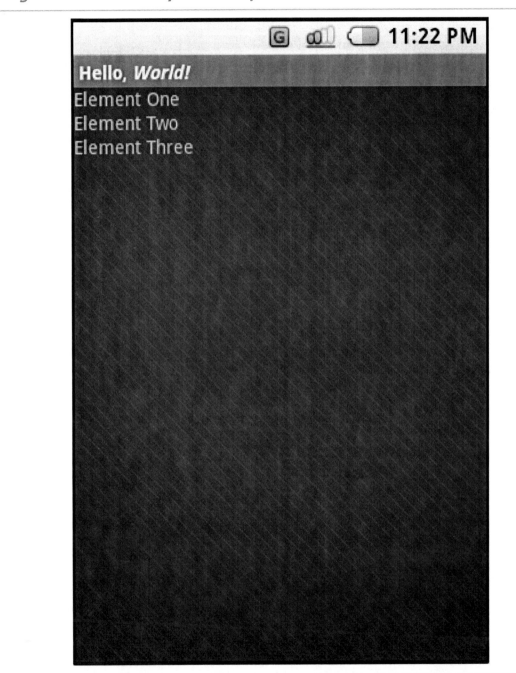

RelativeLayout

Each child element is laid out in relation to other child elements. Relationships can be established so that children will start themselves where a previous child ends. Children can relate only to elements that are listed before them. So, build your dependency from the beginning of the XML file to the end. Note that IDs are required so that widgets can reference each other. For example (see Figure 3-2):

```
<RelativeLayout xmlns:android=
    "http://schemas.android.com/apk/res/android"
android:layout_width="fill_parent"
    android:layout_height="fill_parent"
>
<TextView
    android:id="@+id/EL01"
    android:layout_width="wrap_content"
    android:layout_height="wrap_content"
    android:text="Element One"
    />
<TextView
    android:id="@+id/EL02"
    android:layout_width="wrap_content"
    android:layout_height="wrap_content"
    android:text="Element Two"
    android:layout_below="@id/EL01"
    />
<TextView
        android:layout_width="wrap_content"
    android:layout_height="wrap_content"
    android:text="Element Three"
    android:layout_toRight="@id/EL02"
    />
</RelativeLayout>
```

Figure 3-2. Relative layout example

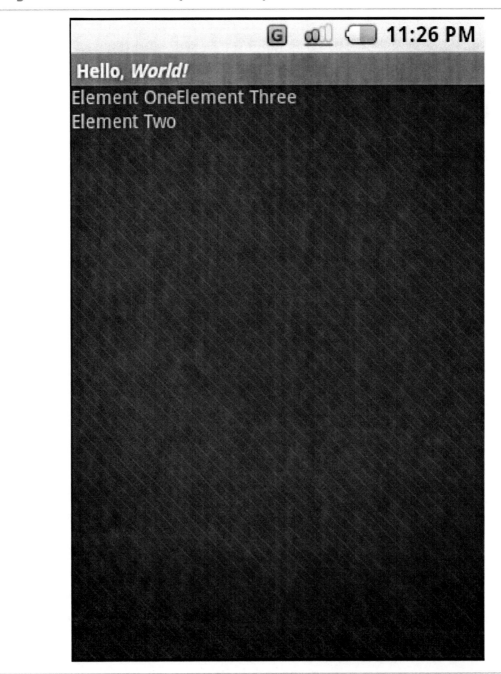

AbsoluteLayout

Each child must be given a specific location within the bounds of the parent layout object. The AbsoluteLayout object is probably the easiest to build and visualize but the hardest to migrate to a new device or screen size. For example (see Figure 3-3):

```
<AbsoluteLayout xmlns:android=
    "http://schemas.android.com/apk/res/android"
    android:layout_width="fill_parent"
    android:layout_height="fill_parent"
>
<TextView
    android:layout_width="wrap_content"
    android:layout_height="wrap_content"
    android:text="Element One"
    />
<TextView
    android:layout_width="wrap_content"
    android:layout_height="wrap_content"
    android:text="Element Two"
    android:layout_x="30px"
    android:layout_y="30px"
    />
<TextView
    android:layout_width="wrap_content"
    android:layout_height="wrap_content"
    android:text="Element Three"
    android:layout_x="50px"
    android:layout_y="50px"
    />
</AbsoluteLayout>
```

Figure 3-3. Absolute layout example

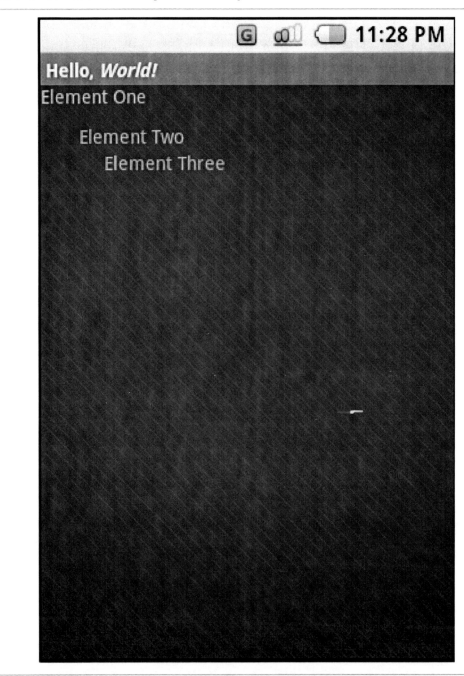

TableLayout

`TableLayout` is a layout object that allows you to specify table rows. Android tries to arrange each of the child elements into the correct row and columns. For example (see Figure 3-4):

```
<TableLayout xmlns:android=
    "http://schemas.android.com/apk/res/android"
    android:layout_width="fill_parent"
    android:layout_height="fill_parent">

<TableRow>
    <TextView
    android:layout_width="wrap_content"
    android:layout_height="wrap_content"
    android:text="Element One A"
    />
    <TextView
    android:layout_width="wrap_content"
    android:layout_height="wrap_content"
    android:text="Element One B"
    />
    </TableRow>
    <TableRow>
    <TextView
    android:layout_width="wrap_content"
    android:layout_height="wrap_content"
    android:text="Element Two A"
    />
    <TextView
    android:layout_width="wrap_content"
    android:layout_height="wrap_content"
    android:text="Element Two B"
    />
    </TableRow>
</TableLayout>
```

Figure 3-4. Table layout example

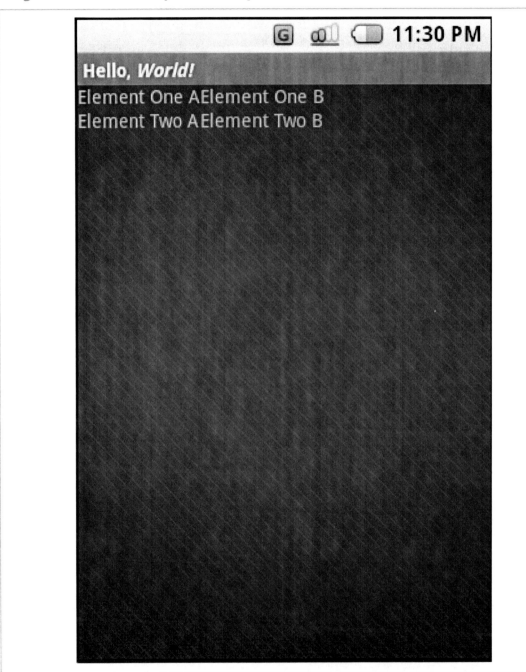

These are the major layout objects you'll be using as you go forward. Each example has a few simple `TextView` elements to demonstrate how the layout shakes down for each layout type and a screen capture depicting how each XML file will render. You can find more thorough examples in the Android documentation at `http://code.google.com/android/samples/ApiDemos/src/com/google/android/samples/view/`.

Note If you're new to mobile development, when deciding how to lay out your application, you must repeat one motto in your head: "porting, porting, porting." Ideally, one layout could be set up that would work for all possible devices. In reality, this never works. If you plan on running your application on more than one phone (as most carriers require that you do), put an emphasis on dynamic and relative layout structures. I promise, your screen size will change in a dramatic way later. Minimize the number of absolute X/Y values, and keep the ones you do use in easy-to-find locations.

The next task is finding a list of all the relevant child elements that can be placed inside a layout. This resource is available in confusing documentation form at `http://code.google.com/android/reference/android/R.styleable.html#Menu`.

From there, you can move on to the first UI task: making a login screen for the "socially awkward" application. This login screen will become part of the `getSplashy` example application.

Scrolling, Text Entry, Buttons, and All the Simple Things in Life

It's now time to put one of the layout classes to use. XML layouts are perfect for user input, information relay, and nearly anything where the contents of the screen are relatively static. You'll add a simple login screen to the aforementioned "socially awkward" application (see Code Listing 3-1). The first task is to describe what the screen will look like in a new view. You'll use a linear layout so you can just add widgets vertically. (Note that this XML requires a `general_bg` image and the disclaimer string to be defined in the `res` folder. Download the project for this chapter from the Apress web site for more information.)

Code Listing 3-1. `/res/layout/login.xml`

```
<ScrollView xmlns:android=
    "http://schemas.android.com/apk/res/android"
    android:layout_width="fill_parent"
    android:layout_height="wrap_content"
    android:scrollbars="vertical">

<LinearLayout
    android:orientation="vertical"
    android:layout_width="fill_parent"
    android:layout_height="fill_parent"
    android:background="@drawable/general_bg"
>

    <TextView
    android:text="Login Screen"
    android:layout_width="fill_parent"
    android:layout_height="wrap_content"
    android:textAlign="center"
    />
    <TextView
    android:text="Username:"
    android:layout_width="wrap_content"
    android:layout_height="wrap_content"
    />
    <EditText
    android:id="@+id/username"
     android:layout_width="fill_parent"
android:layout_height="wrap_content"
    />
```

```xml
<TextView
    android:text="Password:"
    android:layout_width="wrap_content"
    android:layout_height="wrap_content"
/>
<EditText
    android:id="@+id/password"
    android:layout_width="fill_parent"
    android:layout_height="wrap_content"
    />
<Button
    android:id="@+id/loginbutton"
    android:layout_width="wrap_content"
android:layout_height="wrap_content"
android:text="Login"
/>
<TextView
    android:id="@+id/status"
    android:layout_width="fill_parent"
    android:layout_height="wrap_content"
    android:textAlign="center"
    android:text="Enter Username and Password"
    />
    <TextView
    android:layout_width="fill_parent"
    android:layout_height="wrap_content"
    android:text="@string/disclaimer"
    />

</LinearLayout>
</ScrollView>
```

I'll pull a few specific lines from the previous listing and explain what they do in the following sections. Remember, you haven't defined any locations for the elements that make up this screen. However, because you're using the LinearLayout object, each successive element is attached to the bottom of the previous element.

Scrolling

To scroll through a view that's grown larger than the size of your device's screen, simply wrap your layout object in a `ScrollView`. To enable scroll bars vertically, your `ScrollView` must set the parameter `android:scrollbars="vertical"`, which will display a scroll bar only as you page down the screen. To make the view long enough to demonstrate this object, I've added a `TextView` with a phony disclaimer to the end of the linear layout. You'll notice that if you set the previous XML as the active view, that focus will shift down the objects until you reach the button, at which point the scroll bar will handle the down key and move the user to the bottom of the text.

Prying Open the TextView

Two major "widgets" are at work in the previous XML.

Note   A *widget* in Android refers to any self-contained subclass of the `View` object.

For the titles and text-entry labels, you use the `TextView` object. For user-controlled text entry, you use the `EditText` object. Most notable, and therefore the one worth going over in more detail, is the final "status" text:

```
<TextView
    android:id="@+id/status"
    android:layout_width="fill_parent"
    android:layout_height="wrap_content"
    android:textAlign="center"
    android:text="Enter Username and Password"
    />
```

First, because this text element is going to be modified at some point by your source code at runtime, you need to give it an ID. This allows you to use the `findViewById` method later to get a handler for it.

The @+id/status will add the ID status to your R.java file if it doesn't exist already. This might bug out your IDE when you reference it in your code for the first time. Never fear, though, because the first time you compile, all will be sorted out.

Next, you tell the TextView to set its width to the width of its parent, in this case, the LinearLayout object. You tell it to let its height be bounded by the size of the text by using wrap_content for the layout_height parameter. You want the text to reside in the center of the screen, so you'll use textAlign because you've set its width to be the entire screen. Lastly, you'll give it some simple text to display when the activity starts up. Later, you'll change this text to reflect the current status.

To see the results of this handiwork, simply create an activity, and set this XML layout to be the main content view. You should be able to see the screen, type in the text entry field, and select the box. These actions, however, will have no results. To tie them into the program and make them interactive, you'll have to keep reading.

XML Layout

The take-home message here is that the XML layout scheme is both simple and powerful. It provides a nonprogrammer interface for mobile screen layout and design. It also gives developers the tools to crack open and modify these values on the fly during runtime, as you'll do now by exploring how to interact with Android's built-in widgets.

Waking Up the Widgets

I've already demonstrated how to use Android's TextView, Button, and EditText widgets. But how useful is a text-entry field if you can't ingest what your users have entered? That's a rhetorical question; don't answer it—I won't be able to hear you (I hope). The answer is obvious: text entry with no purpose or result is not useful at all. To access the contents of the EditText widgets you defined earlier, you'll have to do two things:

1. Get an object handle to the widget you defined in the XML.

2. Listen for clicks or select events on the Login button widget.

Getting a Handle on Things

The first task is to get a pointer to elements you've defined in your XML layout files. To do this, you'll make sure that each XML widget you want to access has an android:id parameter. As briefly mentioned earlier, using the notation @+id/-id_name_here- will make sure your R.java file has the ID you need. The following is an example of how to get a pointer to the View object when your application starts up. This is the onCreate method in your new login activity added to the GetSplashy example application:

```
Button btn = null;
public void onCreate(Bundle args)
{
    super.onCreate(args);
    setContentView(R.layout.login);

    btn = (Button) findViewById(R.id.loginbutton);
}
```

Here you've acquired a pointer to the login button by calling findViewById. This allows you to add a click listener so that you'll be notified when the button is selected (on a touch screen with a stylus) or selected by the center softkey. You'll extend the ClickListener class inline as follows:

```
public class loginScreen extends Activity
{

    private OnClickListener buttonListener =
        new OnClickListener()
```

```
    {
        public void onClick(View v)
        {
            grabEnteredText();
        }
    };
    ...
}
```

The previous inline definition, when notified that a selection has occurred, calls the `grabEnteredText` method. Now that you've defined the click listener, you can use the `btn` reference in the `onCreate` method:

```
public void onCreate(Bundle args)
{
    //...

    btn = (Button) findViewById(R.id.loginbutton);
    btn.setOnClickListener(buttonListener);
}
```

If you place a breakpoint in your button listener's `onClick` method, it should fire both when you move focus to and select the login button and when you click it with your mouse while running the emulator.

Reeling in the Text

All that's left to do is to define `grabEnteredText` to do exactly as its name implies. In the final production version of a login screen, you want to extract the entered text, begin a network login call, and fire up a loading dialog box. For now, you'll just show a dialog box containing what's been entered in the login and password fields. Here's what `grabEnteredText` looks like in the updated login activity:

```
public void grabEnteredText()
{
    //Get a pointer to the status text
    TextView status =
        (TextView) findViewById(R.id.status);
```

```
//Grab handles to both text-entry fields
EditText username =
  (EditText) findViewById(R.id.username);
EditText pwd =
  (EditText) findViewById(R.id.password);

//Extract Strings from the EditText objects
// and format them in strings
String usrTxt = username.getText().toString();
String pwdTxt = pwd.getText().toString();

//HTTP transaction would spin up a
//new thread here
status.setText("Login" + usrTxt + " : " + pwdTxt);

//Show dialog box that would eventually turn into
this.showAlert("Login Data", 0, "Login"
    + usrTxt + " : " + pwdTxt, "ok!", false);
}
```

First, using findViewById, you retrieve TextView and EditText pointers for the status, username, and password widgets. Next, you extract the contents of the text-entry widgets by retrieving the TextEntry object and converting it into a String class. Last, you put the contents of the two fields together, add both of them to the status text object, and pop up a dialog box also containing the two strings.

That's it—you've now allowed a user to enter text, and you've grabbed, manipulated, and even displayed a dialog box containing that information. Well done! Take a second to pat yourself, or anyone who might happen to be within arms reach, on the back.

So far, you've explored how to do screen layout in XML alone with the "socially awkward" splash screen. You've learned how to use a hybrid of the two just now with your login screen. The last stop on the Android widget express will require building onscreen layouts using code alone.

Widgets in Java

When you see the amount of code I've written to produce even a small selectable menu, you'll probably be, like I was, somewhat aghast. After getting the hang of screen layout in XML, trying to do it all by hand in Java will feel like playing classical music on the piano with a pair of scuffed-up bowling balls. Be warned—it involves a lot of typing and probably more than a little frustration.

On the other hand, there may be some specific elements of a UI layout you want to adjust dynamically at runtime. Since, as I've mentioned earlier, you cannot edit the layout XML files when the application is run, it's essential to have the tools required to modify every possible piece of the user interface in code at runtime. Android gives you that power, provided you're comfortable typing at blazing speeds.

Getting Under the Hood

You'll now tinker under the hood and kick the tires of Android's widgets. You'll take a basic look at some of the core pieces, many of which you've explored in XML form. As in previous examples, for the sake of explanation, I'll keep it basic. It should be easy to apply what I've discussed here to the more complicated aspects of UI layout. In later, more advanced examples, you'll get more into other Android widgets. In the following example, I've taken pains to make sure you use little to none of the XML elements you relied on previously. It should give you a chance to get a good handle on non-XML layout, but keep in mind, practically, you'd have to be crazy to do all your user interface screens this way.

The Main Menu

Nearly all mobile applications, at least at the time of publication, begin with a graphical main menu. This graphical screen directs users to the various functionality of the mobile application. Because the concept of a "main menu" is so universal to the mobile application experience, it makes for an excellent and practical case study. Your objective, in this example, is to put together a simple and functional main menu. For the sake of comparison, you'll use another linear layout to put everything together. The example will be built in three major stages:

1. *Layout*: You'll arrange all the entries of your main menu correctly on the screen. Granted, this will use only a fraction of Android's massive screen real estate. But most application menus will use large graphics and take up significantly more space.

2. *Focus*: You'll need to set up a focus structure so that users can move through the elements. As the focus shifts, you'll have to adjust the colors of each menu element.

3. *Select events*: Finally, you'll need to set up a listener so that when an element is selected or clicked, you're informed and can take the appropriate action based on the item selected.

When you've finished all three of these tasks, you should have the framework to build the primary entry screen of about 80 percent of all mobile applications. Although not entirely practical (being that I've used exactly zero XML), it is an excellent demonstration of how to get things done in a custom runtime-driven way. As you add more functionality to your "socially awkward" application, you'll fill out this main menu more completely.

Laying Out, Java-Style

The first step in the simple main menu is getting all your menu elements on the screen. As I mentioned earlier, you'll be using a linear layout to accomplish it. You'll need to do all this before the application draws for the first time, so it'll have to be in the onCreate method of the new MainMenu activity. (Refer to Chapter 1 if you've lost track of how to create and plug in a new activity.) Code Listing 3-2 shows what its instantiation and configuration looks like.

```
LinearLayout layout = new LinearLayout(this);
layout.setBackground(R.drawable.general_bg);
layout.setOrientation(LinearLayout.VERTICAL);
layout.setLayoutParams(
    new LayoutParams(LayoutParams.FILL_PARENT,
        LayoutParams.FILL_PARENT));
setContentView(layout);
```

After what you've been through thus far, this, conceptually, should seem familiar. You'll set the background using an image in the `/res/drawable/` folder, set the linear layout orientation to vertical, and set the `LayoutParams` to fill the parent. (The parent, in this case, is the activity, which controls the full screen.) Layout parameters, at their base, must define the height and width of a given widget. As you'll probably find out later, trying to place a widget into a `ViewGroup` before its layout parameters are set will throw an exception. However, now that you have a layout object to fill, you can start building out the screen.

Adding a Title

Next, add a simple title, which will be centered, at the top of your main menu screen. Code Listing 3-3 shows the block of code you'll need for it.

Code Listing 3-3. Adding the Title

```
TextView title = new TextView(this);
title.setText(R.string.man_menu_title);
title.setLayoutParams(
        new LinearLayout.LayoutParams(
        LinearLayout.LayoutParams.FILL_PARENT,
        LayoutParams.WRAP_CONTENT));
title.setAlignment(Alignment.ALIGN_CENTER);

layout.addView(title);
```

Create the text object, and set the text from the `/res/values/strings.xml`. I know I said I wouldn't use any XML, but

I'm afraid I may have fibbed about that bit. In production, you'll want to move all your strings to this location rather than defining them in code. If your clients are like mine, you won't want to pull out your source editor and recompile every time they want to change the wording on one of the screens.

Now that you have a title, it's time to add the more interesting and active menu elements.

Laying Out Menu Entries

Now you'll add the individual menu elements. Because this is going to be fairly repetitive after the first one, I'll insert and explain the first element but leave you to your own devices for the rest. Feel free to grab the full project at the Apress site to see the rest of the menu items. Again, you'll fill in more of them as you progress through the rest of the Android essentials. Code Listing 3-4 shows the code to add an individual menu item.

Code Listing 3-4. Adding a Menu Item

```
TextView ItemOne = new TextView(this);
ItemOne.setFocusable(true);
ItemOne.setText("Login Screen");
ItemOne.setTextColor(Color.WHITE);
ItemOne.setLayoutParams(
new LinearLayout.LayoutParams(
LinearLayout.LayoutParams.FILL_PARENT,
        LayoutParams.WRAP_CONTENT));

//Give the menu item an ID for tracking reasons.
//The ID is a static int defined locally to the class
ItemOne.setId(IdOne);
//Add it to our linear layout
layout.addView(ItemOne);
```

Gosh, you probably think after reading the code carefully, this looks almost like the title you've already added. You're exactly right, how clever of you. The heavy lifting of denoting when an object is in focus and when it's been selected has yet to come, so don't get too cocky yet. Here are the two differences between the previous menu item and previously listed title text:

- You need to tell the `TextView` that it can accept focus by calling the `setFocusable` method.

- The menu listing item will need an ID so you can distinguish it from the rest of the menu elements in your selection handler.

As I mentioned briefly, whenever adding a widget to a `ViewGroup`, the `LayoutParams` object must specifically be the object defined within that view group. For example, in the previous `setLayoutParams` method call, you must pass in a `LinearLayout.LayoutParams` object. You must pass in the correct subclassed layout parameter, or Android will throw an exception at you during runtime.

As I said before, to make the menu, I'll add two more text elements almost exactly like the previous listing. For the sake of expediency, I won't list them here. Be sure to refer to the full project to satisfy your curiosity. Now that you have all your menu items in place, it's time to modify them when they receive or lose focus.

Focus Young Grasshopper....

To handle focus change events, you have to create an implementation of the `OnFocusChangeListener` abstract class. The example's version, defined locally within the `MainMenu` activity class, will look like Code Listing 3-5.

Code Listing 3-5. Creating a Focus Listener

```
OnFocusChangeListener focusListener =
    new OnFocusChangeListener()
{
    public void onFocusChanged(View v, boolean hasFocus)
    {
        adjustTextColor(v, hasFocus);
    }
```

```
};
private void adjustTextColor(View v, boolean hasFocus)
{
    //Dangerous cast.  Be sure you are
    //listening only to TextView focus changes
    // or this could go horribly wrong.
    TextView t = (TextView)v;
    if(hasFocus)
        t.setTextColor(Color.RED);
    else
        t.setTextColor(Color.WHITE);
}
```

In addition, you have to add the following line corresponding to each selectable element in the menu to attach the focus change listener object:

```
ItemOne.setOnFocusChangeListener(focusListener);
```

With the listener in place, you'll now be notified each time one of your menu elements gains or loses focus. In more advanced main menus, this method would be the place to add image shifts, animations, 3D explosions, or other whiz-bang graphical effects. In this example, you'll have to settle for just changing the text color. Now that the user can tell, through the color change, which menu item is highlighted, you'll need to react when they press the center key to select an item.

Tip   It's possible to set the focused, unfocused, and selected color of a `TextView` by using the `setTextColor(ColorStateList colors)` method, which is a simpler way of implementing a text-based main menu. There are always many ways to accomplish a goal in a good IDE; I've simply selected the more versatile (because I hope your applications move beyond text menus). For more information on using `setTextColor`, see the Android documentation at `http://code.google.com/android/reference/android/widget/TextView.html#setTextColor(int)`.

Click and Select Events

You've already seen how to register for onClick events in the login screen, so you should be able to breeze through this section without trouble. Code Listing 3-6 shows the example code to grab select events.

Code Listing 3-6. Adding a Selection Listener

```
OnClickListener clickListener = new OnClickListener()
{
    public void onClick(View v)
    {
        String text = "You selected Item: ";
        switch(v.getId())
        {
        case IdOne:
            text += "1";
            startActivity(
             new Intent(MainMenu.this, Login.class));
            break;
        case IdTwo:
            text += "2";
            startActivity(
                new Intent(
                "com.apress.example.CUSTOM_VIEW"));
            break;
        case IdThree:
            text += "3";
            break;
        }
        //We'll get to the following line in a bit
        status.setText(text);
    }
};
```

The previous switch statement is the reason for calling setID back when you were originally creating and laying out the TextView widgets. When a menu item is selected or clicked by the pointer, the onClick function is called, and the corresponding view is passed in as a parameter. You will examine the ID of the view passed in to determine which menu item was selected. This allows you to take the appropriate action for the menu selected. In this way, you can switch to the previously defined login screen and your soon-to-be-written custom view with the `startActivity` method call.

There's still one small step left, and if you look at the bottom of the `onCreatefuction` in the sample code, you'll spot it. You need to add a click listener to the view. Here's the line that should be run while you build up the widget list:

```
ItemOne.setOnClickListener(clickListener);
```

Looking Back

Reviewing the Java-driven main menu, you've accomplished several important things.

First, you performed the layout functionally previously only through XML files. Although not entirely practical to do by hand, it does give you the tools to change and customize the XML views while your application is running.

Second, you registered for focus change events for all your menu items. When the focus change listener was called, you changed the color of the focused item to highlight it. In practical use, there are more efficient ways of accomplishing the same thing, but I'm assuming you'd want to substitute changing text colors for something more, shall we say, extravagant.

Third, you learned how to listen for and react to select events, discern which item was selected, and take the appropriate action based on that selection.

Again, looking over all the code required to lay widgets out on the screen by hand is fairly prohibitive, but using the tools you've just learned, you could modify, enhance, and customize how a menu or list works based on data and user preference while the app is running. If, however, you need to get even more specialized with how you draw to the screen, you'll need a less subtle and more code-heavy approach.

Custom UI Rendering with the Canvas

This is the section all you budding game developers have been waiting for. Android allows you to define a custom `View` object simply by extending the `View` class and implementing the `onDraw` method. To demonstrate a custom view running in an animation loop, I've taken some inspiration from a San Francisco Exploratorium exhibit about how we perceive motion and sound. You can find more information on the museum and the relevant exhibit at `http://www.exploratorium.edu/listen/index.php`. You can purchase the scientific white paper at `http://www.nature.com/neuro/journal/v7/n7/full/nn1268.html`.

The example will animate two balls traveling toward each other and then either passing by or bouncing and moving away. The example is meant to show that the sound of a bounce can make the difference between a person seeing the objects pass and seeing them bounce off each other. Code-wise, I'll demonstrate a few essential aspects of a custom view:

- Implementing an Android view
- Drawing to the screen using the `Canvas` object
- Creating an animation loop
- Modifying and interacting with your custom view from the activity

Customizing the View

You can customize view windows in two ways. The first is to extend the `View` class. This allows you to roll your own "widget" by creating a viable child class of `android.View`. The other method, which you'll have to explore on your own, is to subclass an existing widget such as `TextView`, `ProgressBar`, or `ImageView` and modify its behavior using protected methods. This example shows the first option because its scope is broad and a little easier to understand.

At its most basic level, a custom widget overrides the protected `onDraw` method. Code Listing 3-7 shows an example of just such a method.

Code Listing 3-7. Simple Custom `View` Declared in the `CanvasExample` Activity

```
protected class CustomView extends View
{
    public void onDraw(Canvas canvas)
    {
        Paint p = new Paint();
        p.setColor(Color.WHITE);
        canvas.drawText("Yo!", 0, 25, p);
    }
}
```

Congratulations! By typing these few lines of text, you're now the proud owner of your own custom widget. Granted, all it does is say hello like my 17-year-old punk cousin, but I suppose you have to start somewhere. For those of you with experience in dealing with the `GameCanvas` object in Java ME, this should look familiar. To receive `onDraw` calls, you'll need to set it as the main content view for the sample activity. You'll have to write code that will instantiate it and make it the current view. Code Listing 3-8 shows what the `CanvasExample` activity will look like.

Code Listing 3-8. Activating a Custom View

```
CustomView vw = null;
public void onCreate(Bundle args)
{
    super.onCreate(args);
    vw = new CustomView(this);
    setTitle("Bounce or Pass, sounds changes everything");
    setContentView(vw);
}
```

You set the title for your sample activity because you haven't given it an application name. Then it's just a matter of creating a new `CustomView` object and setting it to be the current content view. This will call the `onDraw` method within your custom widget and display your somewhat unconventional greeting. You now have a handle on drawing to the screen in a very basic way. You should now be able to get into more complicated rendering and starting your animation loop.

Creating the Game Loop

As all game programmers will tell you, most games, at their core, consist of a constant loop. The loop checks for user input and, based on that input and any other game actions, will then draw the new frame/frames to the screen. The loop in your sample application will not win any awards for complexity or ingenuity, but it will get your started on your own game-rendering loop.

Note   If you want to implement your own animation loop outside the `View`/`ViewGroup` hierarchy, look into building a loop with the `SurfaceView` object. You can find documentation for this object at http://code.google.com/android/reference/android/view/SurfaceView.html.

Loading Audio and Images

Before you get into drawing the `CustomView`, you'll need to load a few resources on initialization that will be used later. Code Listing 3-9 shows the new constructor for `CustomView` including local class variable declarations.

Code Listing 3-9. Initializing the CustomView

```
protected class CustomView extends View
{
    Context ctx;
    Paint lPaint = new Paint();
    int x_1=0,y_1=0;
    MediaPlayer player = null;
    Bitmap ball = null;
    boolean running = true;

    CustomView(Context c)
    {
        super(c);
        player = MediaPlayer.create(c, R.raw.bounce);
        BitmapDrawable d = (BitmapDrawable)
        getResources().getDrawable(R.drawable.theball);
        ball = d.getBitmap();
        ctx = c;
    }
    ...
}
```

In the constructor, you're loading the bounce media resource from its
/res/raw location through the R.java constants file. Because you've
done this before with several other resource types, you should be an old
hand at it. You also need to load in an image that will be drawn as the
"ball." You do this using the resources manager object, which is retrieved
from the Context object. Although you haven't explicitly loaded an image
in code from a resource location before, it should look like almost any
other resource load.

Implementing the Loop, Implementing the Loop, Implementing the...

Without further ado, Code Listing 3-10 shows what the CustomView
object's onDraw method looks like.

```
public void onDraw(Canvas canvas)
{
    //Draw the white background
    Rect rct = new Rect();
    rct.set(0, 0,
        canvas.getBitmapWidth(),
        canvas.getBitmapHeight());
    Paint pnt = new Paint();
    pnt.setStyle(Paint.Style.FILL);
    pnt.setColor(Color.WHITE);
    canvas.drawRect(rct, pnt);

    //Increment the X and Y value for the sprites
    x_1+=2;
    y_1+=2;

    //Reset the loop when the balls drift offscreen.
    if(x_1 >= canvas.getBitmapWidth())
    {
        x_1 = 0;
        y_1 = 0;
    }

    //Draw ball 1
    drawSprint(x_1, y_1, canvas);
    //Draw ball 2
    drawSprint(canvas.getBitmapWidth() - x_1, y_1, canvas);

    if(running)
        invalidate();
}
```

Starting from the top, you'll first white out the background using a paint-style object and a call to `canvas.drawRect`. The paint object, in combination with the `Rectangle` object, will tell the canvas to draw a white box that covers the entire screen. Next, you'll increment the x and y values for your ball sprites. You'll then need to reset them if they've drifted past the bounds of the screen and, finally, draw them with your own `drawSprite` call. Code Listing 3-11 shows the contents of that function.

Code Listing 3-11. Drawing a Bitmap

```
protected void drawSprint(int x, int y, Canvas canvas)
{
    canvas.drawBitmap(ball, x, y, lPaint);
}
```

This function, right now, is simply a straightforward call to the `drawBitmap` method. I've separated out this method only because drawing the sprite in another context might require more functionality than in this simple example. Finally, returning to the `onDraw` function, you'll call `invalidate` only if your `running` flag is `true`. Calling invalidate on a view is Android's preferred way of forcing a redraw. In this case, you'll invalidate yourself, which will call `onDraw`, and the whole process starts over once again. If you simply set the `running` flag to `false` on pause or exit and invalidate it again when resuming, the animation should stay in step with the focus of its parent activity.

Adding and Controlling Sound

Since the auditory illusion requires the ability to turn on and off the sound of the two objects bouncing off each other, you'll need to set up the audio to play as they hit and then build a mechanism for the user to turn that audio on and off.

To play the audio, add the code in Code Listing 3-12 to the previous `onDraw` function since it is also, in effect, the game control loop. When I say "game loop," I'm referring to the `invalidate` call at the end of `onDraw`, which will place a redraw in Android's UI event loop. Keep in mind that `playSound` is a boolean declared just inside the custom view.

Code Listing 3-12. Playing and Reloading Audio

```
if(playSound &&
    canvas.getBitmapWidth() - x_1 -16 == x_1 + 16)
player.start();

if(x_1 >= canvas.getBitmapWidth())
{
    x_1 = 0;
    y_1 = 0;
    player.stop();
    player.release();
    player = MediaPlayer.create(ctx, R.raw.bounce);
}
```

As you might have noticed, you're starting the audio playback when the sprites are 16 pixels away from each other. This is a little slush time to let the audio get started. I should note that it speaks more to my inability to edit audio files than it does to a lack of efficiency in audio load and playback times in Android. You also must be sure to play the audio only if the playSound boolean is true. This variable is a member of the Activity class in which the custom view is defined. Using this boolean, you'll get control over the custom view class from within the screen activity. To turn on and off the audio, you now simply implement the method in Code Listing 3-13 in the activity.

Code Listing 3-13. Reacting to Key Events

```
public boolean onKeyDown(int key, KeyEvent kc)
{
    if(key == KeyEvent.KEYCODE_DPAD_CENTER)
    {
        playSound = !playSound;
        return true;
    }

    return super.onKeyDown(key, kc);
}
```

This code should look similar to how you dismissed the prank application in Chapter 2.

Bringing It All Together

If you've followed along closely (or cheated and simply downloaded the finished project), you should be able to run the application and watch the illusion. Press the center directional key to turn on and off the audio. With the audio off, it should look like they pass each other; with it on, it looks like they bounce off and go their separate ways.

In this example, I've demonstrated how to create your own `View` subclass, how use it to draw on the screen, how to set up a game-rendering loop, and how to control that simple loop using key events.

Using the User Interface

In this chapter, you've learned, in detail, how to lay out screens using Android's XML schema and how to interact and modify that schema at runtime with some Java code.

Next, you learned how lay out UI widgets and view groups using source code alone. It's a not-so-practical application of Android user interface tools, but it's important to go through for the sake of understanding nonetheless. Last, you explored the essential tools for building a game-rendering loop. You added some simple multimedia and user control into the mix and created a simple auditory illusion that should impress your very nerdy friends.

Tip   Using all that you've learned in this chapter, build a frame for this illusion that contains some explanatory text and a border using XML. When the activity starts up, render the XML but insert the custom view into the proper place. For this task, I suggest using a relative layout, a `TextView` for the explanation, and a `Rectangle` for the border.

Chapter 4: Location, Location, Location

In this chapter, we'll tackle the very trendy subject of location-based services. One of Android's major selling points is its native access to the Google Maps infrastructure. Although it is an optional feature, what carrier wouldn't include this powerful package? I suppose that, in the coming year or so, we'll find out. You'll delve into this subject in two major parts in this chapter. First, you'll take on Android's `LocationManager` object, which allows you to determine your latitude and longitude, ostensibly, using a variety of systems under the hood. Next, you'll get into making the Google Maps API do your bidding. It's important to note that Android's support for GPS and tower-based location systems is not fully implemented. At press time, it's possible to emulate GPS data either by using the default, which is a drive around the Bay Area in California, or by building your own fake GPS data. My example will use the first method, but I'll include code that should eventually work with shipping handsets. You can find more information about building a custom GPS route and the ins and outs of location-based services (LBSs) in the Android documentation at `http://code.google.com/android/toolbox/apis/lbs.html`.

By means of example, you'll implement an application that retrieves the handset's location from the sample GPS module, starts a `MapActivity` object, centers the screen on the location, and then uses an overlay to draw a tack on top of it.

Where Am I?

For the most part, location-based services with Android work exactly as you would expect them to with one minor exception. Android allows for developers to specify which location lookup method to use. This allows you to customize the power consumption, cost, and accuracy based on the specific use you have in mind for your application.

Building the LocationManager Object

The first task will be to get a handler to the `LocationManager` object, the high-level object used to find the handset's location. The `LocationManager` can use any number of `LocationProvider` objects to do the GPS (or tower-based) lookup. Here are the relevant class variable declarations and subsequent `buildGPS` method that will prime the pump for later location retrieval:

```
Point m_curLocation;
LocationProvider m_locationProvider;
LocationManager m_locationMgr;

private void buildGPS()
{
    List<LocationProvider> providorList = null;
    Criteria c = new Criteria();

    c.setAccuracy(50);
    c.setAltitudeRequired(false);
    c.setCostAllowed(false);
    c.setSpeedRequired(false);
    //Following line is commented out because it drops
    //android into an infinite loop.
    //c.setPowerRequirement(c.POWER_LOW);

    m_locationMgr =
      (LocationManager)
        getSystemService(LOCATION_SERVICE);

    m_locationProvider = m_locationMgr.getBestProvider(c);

    if(m_locationProvider != null)
        return;

    providorList = m_locationMgr.getProviders();

    if(providorList.size() > 0)
        m_locationProvider = providorList.get(0);
}
```

You'll notice that you can't simply instantiate a new `LocationManager` object. It must be retrieved through the `getSystemService` method, a public member of the `Activity` class.

One Must-Have Standard

Once you've declared the relevant variables, you'll build a useless (at least until Android arrives on devices) `Criteria` object. The `Criteria` allows you to specify features for the lookup method you want to use.

In this example, since you'll be tracking the user constantly in an urban environment, you want something low-cost, low-power, and accurate. You won't need speed or altitude because you're just going to be pushing this information to the Google Maps screen. You'll specify all these variables by making calls to the `Criteria` object, which will eventually be passed into the `LocationManager` object.

With these criteria set, you can request the best provider that meets your needs. Again, because the Android emulator supports only one example GPS stub, you'll get a null object back from the `getBestProvider` call. Later, with real hardware, these criteria will be more effective, even essential. Since the LBS criteria were rejected, you'll just grab the first element of the provider list, which will be named, at least in this version of the Android software, `gps`.

Note, also, that the low-power requirement is commented out. At time of publication, including this setting causes Android to spiral into some kind of infinite loop. Android engineers, heads up!

Look Up, Wave, the Satellites Are Watching...

Now that I've laid the groundwork for your location service, you can move on to the lookup itself. The application will request its coordinates every five seconds and move the containing `MapActivity` to the correct place (something I'll get into at length later in the chapter). Code Listing 4-1 shows the code to start the operation. It won't compile until you include the code that comes in the next block after this one, because you'll have to define the `LocationUpdater` object.

Code Listing 4-1. Registering for Location Updates

```
boolean running = true;
private void startLocationThread()
{
    try
    {
        LocationUpdater l = new LocationUpdater();
        registerReceiver(l,
            new IntentFilter("GPS_UPDATE"));

        m_locationMgr.requestUpdates(
            m_locationProvider, 5000,
            50, new Intent("GPS_UPDATE")
    } catch (Exception e){}
}
```

To download the location at five-second intervals, you'll request updates from the location manager. First, you'll have to register a new `LocationUpdater` for the `GPS_UPDATE` intent. This is the intent that will be fired each time the `LocationManager` has an update for you.

Tip   It's a good idea to request updates in the `onResume` activity method and to stop the updates when `onPause` is called. This keeps your application from consuming resources while your application is not the topmost visible application.

You can specify which provider (on the emulator it'll be `gps`, but on the handset it'll be the closest location provider to your specifications) and specify the time interval as 5000 and max distance change as 50 meters. Remember, both of these qualifications need to be met for a `GPS_UPDATE` intent to be fired.

Of course, for this code to work, you'll have to define what a
LocationUpdater is. You'll define it within the example activity so it has
access to the activity's private members; see Code Listing 4-2.

Code Listing 4-2. Defining the Intent Receiver

```
class LocationUpdater extends IntentReceiver
    {
        public void onReceiveIntent(
            Context context, Intent intent)
        {
            Location here;

            if (m_locationProvider == null)
                here =
                    m_locationMgr.
                    getCurrentLocation("gps");
            else
                here =
                    m_locationMgr.
                    getCurrentLocation(
                    m_locationProvider.getName());

            setMapLocationCenter(
                here.getLatitude(),
                here.getLongitude());
        }
    };
```

In the previous code, the onReceiveIntent function is called when the
LocationManager sends out a GPS_UPDATE intent. When you're notified
of a five-second interval (or a 500-meter location change), you'll acquire a
new location and call setMapLocationCenter to update the location of
the phone on the Google Maps object.

So, you now have the latitude and longitude of the handset coming in every
five seconds. You have the location, so let's write some code to display
that information on a map.

Note   Don't forget to add the correct permissions to your manifest file when requesting LBS data. You'll want to add ACCESS_LOCATION, ACCESS_GPS, ACCESS_CELL_ID, and ACCESS_ASSISTED_GPS. The top-level one will give you access to location services in general. Each of the other permissions will let you access a particular method of location tracking. Be sure to include the ACCESS_LOCATION and at least one other type in your manifest, or your LocationProvider will always come back as null.

Google Maps

It is impossible to write a book about Android without tackling this subject. Developers everywhere salivate at the possibilities made available with a GPS-enabled handset and a native implementation of Google Maps. The fact that you've probably flipped to this chapter and are reading it first should say something about what we're all excited about.

A Metric Ton of Map Objects

You have several players to deal with when displaying a Google Maps screen. It's good to have a quick introduction to all the major players. You'll need to coordinate them all in a delicate ballet of complexity in order to make the map screen behave itself.

- MapActivity is the grand poobah of the Google Maps family. MapActivity takes care of all the low-level thread management, networking, and basic gesture/key handling.

- MapView is the view that supports and displays the map. This must be contained by a MapActivity.

- MapController is the object used to move the map around the screen.

- OverlayController is the superobject to manage all the individual overlay graphics.

- `Overlay` is a single drawable object to be painted overtop the `MapView`.

- `Point` is a single latitude-longitude position. This is the object you'll use to keep track of where the handset is.

Each of the objects listed (yes, there are a lot of them, and no, there will not be a quiz later) plays a significant role in drawing the map and indicating the user's location. Obviously, you'll need to start with the `MapActivity`, because it's the baseline that contains all the rest. Here's the declaration and classwide variable list:

```
public class MapExampleActivity extends MapActivity
{
    MapView m_mapView;
    MapController m_mapController;
    Point m_curLocation;
    LocationProvider m_locationProvider;
    LocationManager m_locationMgr;
    OverlayController m_overlayController;
    boolean m_locationLoopActive = false;
```

Some of these variables should look familiar from the code in the previous location example. I've listed them here just so that you'll have some context for what's to come. Here's the `onCreate` method that will initialize the metric ton of mapping objects:

```
public  void onCreate(Bundle ice)
{
    super.onCreate(ice);
    m_mapView = new MapView(this);
    m_mapController = m_mapView.getController();
    m_overlayController =
        m_mapView.createOverlayController();
    m_overlayController.add(new TackOverlay(this), true);
    m_mapController.zoomTo(9);
    buildGPS();

    setContentView(m_mapView);
}
```

Creating a `MapView`, as you can see, requires nothing more than a context pointer. However, if you try to set it as the content view in something other than a `MapActivity`, you'll find yourself in exception land. The `MapController`, which is what you'll use to move the map to your GPS locations, is retrieved from the `MapView` object. You'll create an `OverlayController` with the `MapView` and add a new instance of your `TackOverlay` object to it.

Keep that `TackOverlay` line in the back of your head until later. You'll return to it in just a minute. Last, you set the zoom level to something that will let you see highways and cites. You'll also need to set up the GPS variables that were covered and listed in the previous section. After all that, you can finally set the `MapView` as the `activeContent` view.

Note   A `MapActivity` can contain more than just a `MapView` object. You can define it and other widgets by hand or through XML, as discussed in Chapter 3. For the most part, the `MapActivity` is exactly like an `Activity` class...aside from its extra resource and thread handling for the `MapView` object.

If you run your `MapActivity` as it stands thus far, you'll see Google Maps start up and center you somewhere in Tulsa, Oklahoma. You'll need to refer to the Android engineers for why it happens that way; I'm frankly at a loss for why you'd want to start your map there, but maybe I just haven't spent enough time in Tulsa.

Moving the Map

Let's look at the code that will move the map to the appropriate location. If you remember your location lookup loop (say that five times fast!), you'll remember the method call:

```
"setMapLocationCenter(
     here.getLatitude(), here.getLongitude());"
```

Since this is the next step in the application, let's take a look at the contents of this simple method:

```
public void setMapLocationCenter(double lat, double lon)
{
    m_curLocation = new Point((int)(lat * 1E6),
        (int) (lon * 1E6));

    m_mapController.animateTo(m_curLocation);
}
```

Now you see the use of the illustrious com.google.android.maps.Point object, not to be confused with the android.graphics.Point object, which is, clearly, difficult to do, because their names are so distinct. The map Point object allows you to set its location with the constructor in 1E6 notation (which, if you're not a mapping/GPS buff, means multiplying the stuff returned from the GPS module by 1E6 to avoid looking like you're somewhere off the coast of Africa).

Now that you've converted the GPS output into a map Point, you can move the onscreen map to center on it. You accomplish this through the map controller by calling animateTo.

The final step in this section is to start the location loop when the user presses the center key. By now, you should be a pro at this sort of thing; in fact, I'll bet you're so good I don't even have to explain the following code:

```
public boolean onKeyDown(int KeyCode, KeyEvent evt)
{
    super.onKeyDown(KeyCode, evt);
    switch(KeyCode)
    {
    case KeyEvent.KEYCODE_DPAD_CENTER:
        if(!m_locationLoopActive)
        {
            m_locationLoopActive = true;
```

```
                startLocationThread();
        }
        return true;
    break;
    }

  return false;
  }
```

Taking Stock

If you've followed along thus far, you should see, when you press the center key, that the map moves to a location in the Bay Area near San Francisco. Additionally, over time, the map will move in parallel with the movement of the fictional handset. Congratulations—if your application were running on a real phone, you'd be looking down at the top of your head…figuratively.

If you cheated and downloaded the example code, 5 points for ingenuity but 20 points off for lack of creativity. You cheaters will notice that a blue tack is drawn at the current location of the handset (the center of the screen if you haven't moved the map around by clicking your mouse). This blue tacky-blobby thing, aside from being a testament to my poor Photoshop skills, is the final part of the Google Maps example. Half the fun of displaying a map is marking things on it. This example, because this book is called *Android Essentials* and not *I'll Write Your Mobile Application for You, OK?*, will be straightforward and simple. You'll draw a tack overlay on the current user's position.

It's a Bird, It's a Plane...Nope, It's Bad Photoshoping

Correctly rendering an overlay is a little more complicated than you might think at first. It requires two major components, the `OverlayController` object and an extended `Overlay` object. The overlay controller manages each overlay and ensures that its `draw` function is called after the `MapView` redraws itself. If you'll recall, and I'll insert it here because you **probably** don't want to, you had to create an overlay controller in the `onCreate` method. Here's the line:

```
m_overlayController =
    m_mapView.createOverlayController();
```

Each drawable `Overlay` must be added to the `OverlayController`. Again, here's the line you used earlier in the example:

```
m_overlayController.add(new TackOverlay(this), true);
```

The `TackOverlay` is an extension of the `Overlay` object. Anytime you want to draw your own "tack," you'll have to extend the `Overlay` object. Granted, one custom `Overlay` with a little efficient creative programming could draw all your overlays. For the purpose of this example, you'll extend the `Overlay` object and add the required `draw` method. The `draw` method will be called after the map redraws itself. Here's the `TackOverlay` declaration, class variables, and constructor; you'll declare it inline within the `MapActivity` so it has access to your `MapActivity`'s variables and functions:

```
class TackOverlay extends Overlay
{
    MapExampleActivity ctx;
    Bitmap tack;

    TackOverlay(MapExampleActivity c)
    {
        super();
        BitmapDrawable b = (BitmapDrawable)
            c.getResources().
            getDrawable(R.drawable.tack);
        tack = b.getBitmap();
}
```

As you can see, the `TackOverlay` looks like just about any other Android object extension. Using the context pointer, you'll stash aside the tack bitmap resource so you won't have to load it every time when drawing. The code gets a little more interesting when you crack into the `draw` method.

```java
public void draw(Canvas canvas, PixelCalculator calculator,
boolean shadow)
{
    super.draw(canvas, calculator, shadow);
    intxy[] = newint[2];

    try{
        //Convert the center point to an XY coordinate.
        //We could hard-code this,
        //but where's the fun in that?
        if(m_curLocation == null)
            return;

        calculator.getPointXY(m_curLocation, xy);

        inttackX = xy[0] - (tack.getWidth()/2);
        inttackY = xy[1] - (tack.getHeight());

        canvas.drawBitmap(tack ,tackX, tackY, new Paint());
    }
    catch (Exception e)
    {
        Log.e("Crap!");
    }
}
```

There's nothing mind-bending in the previous code. The only tricky bit to keep in mind is that you'll need to translate the latitude/longitude coordinates stored in the m_curLocation Point object into an XY coordinate to draw onscreen. To do this, the Overlay object passes in a PixelCalculator object with the draw method. This object is responsible for giving you an XY coordinate that maps to the latitude/longitude position. Because the TackOverlay object is defined inline within the MapExampleActivity, it has access to the m_curLocation point variable. You'll convert that point into an XY location. Because the tack-blob-thingy's point is at the bottom and middle of the image, you'll have to move it up by the height of the tack resource and left by half the width.

This should put the point of the tack in line with the XY calculated location.

Also worth noting, even though I haven't implemented it, is the existence of the `shadow` boolean. This will tell you whether your overlay should draw a shadow. Ignore it or not; it's up to you.

With that, you've completed the example. You can now draw a somewhat misshapen tack on the map at the GPS location of the phone. Granted, you're drawing a faked stub GPS location, but your new cutting-edge LBS application has to start somewhere.

Wrapping Up

My goal in this chapter was not to provide a soup-to-nuts explanation of all that's available in Google Maps for Android. My hope was to provide you with a framework that will let you explore all those things on your own. I covered how to get the handset's location from the `LocationManager` and how to take those values and convert them into a Google Maps location. Then, I covered how to start up a `MapActivity` and draw a map onscreen. Last, you learned how to animate the map around the country and how to draw an overlay, or tack object.

This should give you a solid foundation for what you might want to do next. I recommend exploring the searching capabilities, drawing multiple overlays, and installing the Google map view inside a frame (possibly with explanations, graphics, or control indicators).

Chapter 5: Taking Android Out for a Walk

In this chapter, you'll move past the basics, loosen the leash, and let Android stretch its legs a little bit. More and more as the mobile software field progresses, it's become less and less possible to make an application that doesn't rely heavily on the Web. In many ways, fully featured Internet access has become one of the essentials in the mobile world. The depth and breadth of Android's network layer makes it impossible to cram into one small chapter of one small book. With this in mind, I'll try to, as I have before, arm you with the basics you'll need to make production-level applications. Along the way, as in previous examples, you'll explore a few tangential pieces of Android's technology.

Starting with the essentials, you'll learn how to use a simple HTTP connection to download, parse, and list the elements of a remote XML file. These elements, in your sample application, will be Internet radio stations contained in a basic XML file. Indeed, your entire sample application will be focused on building a simple Internet radio player. Sadly, the state of Android's streaming audio does not live up to its documentation. So, this chapter will be more of an exercise and less of a fully functioning application.

Loading a List from the Web

To make your snazzy example application, you'll have to fetch, parse, and display a simple list of radio stations. Doing this will require me to cover a range of subjects from HTTP transactions to `ListView`s. Pulling down a list down from the Web and displaying them onscreen is something I find myself, as an engineer on many mobile projects, doing nearly constantly. From pulling down a "friends list" on a social network to a "high score list" from an online game element, there's something universal about downloading, parsing, and displaying a list.

Although I realize you might not be making a streaming music application anytime soon, this example is general enough that it should serve as a guide for both basic network operations and handling selection menus. Also of note is that you're performing almost the same task you did with the custom widget work back in Chapter 3. Frankly, I'm not sure this method is a whole lot easier, but perhaps that's because I'm using it in a fairly rudimentary way and have missed some of the more complicated bits it would help with. In any case, enough gabbing—let's get into the basics of network connectivity.

First Things...First?

Your first task will be to pull the XML file off the server. I've made a simple XML example file (which, in your final application, would be provided by a PHP script or a Java servlet) and hosted it on my web site. Before we get any further, I'll list a few variable declarations you're going to need later. Both for network connectivity and for our eventual selectable list, Code Listing 5-1 shows the class declaration and variable dump.

Code Listing 5-1. Essential Class Variables

```
public class StationPicker extendsActivity {

//Uncomment the next lines after we've
//defined the StationData class
//Vector<StationData> stationListVector =
//new Vector<StationData>();
SAXParser parser = null;
XMLReader reader = null;
//You'll have to check the code for the following line.
//XMLHandler handler = new XMLHandler();
ArrayAdapter<StationData> adapter = null;
```

What you see in the previous listing is the buffet of objects you'll need to complete your little sample application. You have the `Vector` to hold the station list, a SAX parser, a reader, and a handler for XML parsing. Last you have the `ArrayAdapter`, which, at some point, you'll fill with elements to render for your onscreen menu.

Additionally, Code Listing 5-2 shows how things are initialized within your `onCreate` function.

Code Listing 5-2. Setting Up for XML Parsing

```
{
    super.onCreate(icicle);
    try
    {
        //This can be just about
        //anything at this point
        setContentView(R.layout.main);
        SAXParserFactory f =
            SAXParserFactory.newInstance();
        parser = f.newSAXParser();
        reader = parser.getXMLReader();
        reader.setContentHandler(handler);
        //We'll get to the contents of the
        //following function later.
        // If you're following along
        //just stub it to return null
        initList();
    }
    catch (Exception e)
    {
        Log.e("StationPicker", "Parser FAIL!");
    }
```

}Again, because I'm assuming you're comfortable with Java, I'm not going to walk through all the steps required. If you want the full context and associated code, feel free to grab the project online. As for the `initList` method, I'll define that in a later section. For now, if you're following along, you can follow the comment's advice and stub it to return `null`.

Getting the Network in Gear

I've elected to kick off the network connection during the `onStart` method inside the `ListActivity`. Normally you would probably do this once on startup and then, using an intent, move to a new activity for showing the list. But for the sake of keeping this example as simple as possible, I'm going to do as much as I can within the single activity. It'll keep you from having to deal with intent management, and it'll give me a chance to show you how to use the UI thread. You'll learn more about that later; for now, the Web! See Code Listing 5-3.

Code Listing 5-3. Creating and Using a Simple HTTP Connection

```
public void onStart()
{
super.onStart();
Thread t = new Thread()
    {
        public void run()
        {
            HttpUriRequest request = null;
            HttpResponse resp = null;
            InputStream is = null;

            DefaultHttpClient client =
                new DefaultHttpClient();

            try{
                //Build the request
                request =
                  new HttpGet(
             "http://www.wanderingoak.net/stations.xml");
                //Execute it using the default
                  //HTTP Client settings;
                resp = client.execute(request);
                //Pull out the entity
                HttpEntity entity= resp.getEntity();
```

```
                //Snag the response stream from the entity
                is = entity.getContent();
                //Parse the incoming data
                reader.parse(new InputSource(is));
            } catch (Exception e)
            {
              Log.e("LoadStations","FAIL!");
            }
        }
    };
    t.start();
}
```

You first need an instance of the `DefaultHttpClient`. You can obtain this by simply creating it with `new`. Next, you'll create a new `HttpGet` object, passing in the location of your XML feed. You can then execute the HTTP request on the default client with your new request object. This is a blocking operation (hence the new thread), and once the execute method returns, you can get the `HttpEntity`. Out of this object you can retrieve an `InputStream` containing the body of the response.

If that final reader call makes no sense to you at all, that's because it shouldn't, because I haven't told you what it does yet. Yes, I know your sample code won't compile without it. Hold on a second, and I'll get to that.

Note   The `DefaultHttpConnection` object seems to spool up and run, at least with the current version of the emulator, hideously slowly. You can probably get better performance by tinkering with the various subclasses of the `HttpClient` class. Your mileage may vary, but if you need a fast and easy proof-of-concept demonstration, the default one may be the way to go.

Putting the Data in Its Place

As you can see in the previous code, pulling down a bit of XML data from a server or any data, for that matter, is a pretty simple process. That `reader.parse` line you've been pestering me about is a simple call to a SAX parser. Android rolls out the door with a few XML parsers to choose from, and since I'm assuming you're comfortable with Java and for the sake of time, I'm not going to spell it out for you.

If you absolutely must know what's going on, you're welcome to grab the sample code and check it out. For now, however, it's enough to know that the parser fills a `Vector` full of `StationData` objects. Code Listing 5-4 shows the definition.

Code Listing 5-4. Defining the Data-Housing Class

```
class StationData
{
    public String title = "";
    public String url = "";
    public String toString()
    {
        return title;
    }
}
```

For simplicity's sake, I've avoided the common encapsulation practice of defining getters and setters on private `String` elements. Instead, you'll just access the elements within the class directly. If you're a C/C++ programmer, this looks more like a "struct" than a "class." Take special note of that `toString` method. It may look useless at this moment, mostly because it is right now, but its function will become much more apparent in a few paragraphs. Each station from the XML file will get its own `StationData` object. Again, just for the sake of example, Code Listing 5-5 shows what a single station element in the XML looks like.

```
<xml>
<stationList>
<station>
<title>Pop Rock Top 40</title>
<audioUrl>
http://scfire-nyk-aa02.stream.aol.com:80/stream/1074
</audioUrl>
</station>
</stationList>
</xml>
```

Since, at this point, you'll let the XML parser take care of things with that `reader.parse` line, you can get on with making your list of selectable elements. Your parser will fill the `StationData` vector with a few elements. Your next few tasks are to pull them out of the vector and place them on the screen in a way the user can interact with.

Making a List and Checking It...

Making your list menu function correctly will require a few steps. You'll first have to convert your activity to a `ListActivity` and do all the housework that switch demands. Next, you'll actually insert the elements from the vector you built previously. Last, you'll react to select events and begin streaming some theoretical audio. Again, in a production version of this application, you would probably use more than one activity, but for the sake of simplicity, you'll just to cram it all into one.

The Setup: Embracing the List

Your first task, if you're going to display the selectable list of stations, is to switch your humdrum activity to a shiny new `ListActivity`. Here's the class declaration in its new and pristine form:

```
public class StationPicker extends ListActivity
```

This conversion carries with it a few notable responsibilities. If you don't fulfill these obligations, Android will throw a bunch of exceptions at you. First, you'll need to add a `ListView` to that default layout file because each `ListActivity` must have an associated `ListView`. Here's what the example `main.xml` looks like:

```xml
<?xml version="1.0" encoding="utf-8"?>
<LinearLayout xmlns:android=
"http://schemas.android.com/apk/res/android"
    android:orientation="vertical"
    android:layout_width="fill_parent"
    android:layout_height="fill_parent"
>
<TextView
    android:layout_width="fill_parent"
    android:layout_height="wrap_content"
    android:text="Loading Stations..."
    android:id="@+id/loadingStatus"
    />
<ListView android:id="@+id/android:list"
        android:layout_width="wrap_content"
        android:layout_height="wrap_content"
        />
</LinearLayout>
```

Adding the Adapter

Second, you'll need to add an adapter to the list widget. You need to define what each element is going to look like. You'll make a simple XML file containing a single text element. Call it `list_element.xml`; it should look like Code Listing 5-6.

Code Listing 5-6. `res/layout/list_element.xml`

```xml
<?xml version="1.0" encoding="utf-8"?>
<TextView id="@+id/textElement"
xmlns:android="http://schemas.android.com/apk/res/android"
android:layout_width="fill_parent"
android:layout_height="wrap_content"/>
```

This `TextView` describes, to Android, what each element in the list should look like. This is the place for fonts, colored texts, and background resources. More complicated list elements are possible, but I'll get into that variation a little bit later.

Remember that `initList` method I told you to stub out earlier? Rather than just returning `null`, Code Listing 5-7 is what it should look like.

Code Listing 5-7. Must Do: Adding an Adapter to the ListView

```
privatevoid initList()
{
    adapter = new ArrayAdapter<StationData>(
        StationPicker.this, R.layout.list_element);
    setListAdapter(adapter);
}
```

Every `ListView` must have a corresponding adapter. Adapters come in a few sizes and flavors. Table 5-1 gives a brief description of the most important among them.

Table 5-1. List Adapters

LIST ADAPTER	DESCRIPTION
Cursor adapter	A simple adapter that is perfect for listing the contents of SQL databases, search results, or any other data that is commonly formatted in a cursor. In fact, the Google documentation has an excellent example of using a cursor adapter: http://code.google.com/android/intro/tutorial -ex1.html.
Resource cursor adapter	The perfect adapter for building a selectable list from a static XML file. If your menu/list is a list of known elements, such as a main menu, list of help topics, or other well-known catalog of information, this is the adapter for you.

continued

Table 5-1. continued

LIST ADAPTER	DESCRIPTION
Array adapter	The adapter we're using in this example. If you don't know what's going to be in your list at compile time, because you won't know what your station list will be, then this is the easiest way to convert a list of XML elements into a selectable list.

For now, you have a fully functioning, while extremely ugly, menu list ready to go. Now all you need is some data!

Stuffing Data into the Adapter

Placing the data in the adapter is simple but for one thing: it must take place inside the UI thread. What, you may ask, am I talking about? The UI thread is a specific thread of execution, which controls the redraw loop. You'll notice that if you start a new generic Java thread and then try to change the current view, add data elements to a list adapter, or any other UI task, Android will get really grumpy with you. By grumpy, I mean it won't work, or it'll throw a stack of exceptions at you.

Reclaiming the UIThread

Since you started a new inline Java thread to handle your blocking network connection, you'll now have to define another "runnable" to get back into the good graces of the UI gods. Thankfully, activities contain a method for scheduling code for the UI thread. You'll add it to the bottom of your network code (see Code Listing 5-8). I'll repeat the last few lines for context.

```
Thread t = new Thread()
{
    //---------
    //Skipping a bunch of
    //Code here
    reader.parse(new InputSource(is));
    //Run our code on the UI Thread.
    UIThreadUtilities.runOnUIThread(
            StationPicker.this,r);
```

Note   Don't try to paste the previous code into your project and compile it just yet. You need to define that runnable `r` object first. Bear with me for just a few minutes, or paragraphs, depending on how fast you read.

The object `UIThreadUtilities` is a mostly static class, which is a member of the `Activity` class. You'll have to pass in a context object to `runOnUIThread`, and since `this` is a pointer to your currently running `Thread` instead of your `ListActivity`, you'll have to grab your `ListActivity` (a subclass of `Context`) from `StationPicker.this`. That `r` reference is a "runnable" that you'll define in just a minute.

At Last, Adding the Data

You're finally ready to start shoveling `StationData` elements into your `ArrayListAdapter`. You'll do that inside that runnable `r` object you heard me talk about earlier (Code Listing 5-9).

Code Listing 5-9. Adding Elements to the Adapter

```
Runnable r = new Runnable()
{
public void run()
{
    TextView t =
        (TextView) findViewById(
            R.id.loadingStatus);
    t.setText("Stations Loaded");
    try{
        for(int i=0;
            i < stationListVector.size();
                i++)
                adapter.addObject(
                stationListVector.elementAt(i));
        }catch (Exception e) {}
            getListView().invalidate();
        }
};
```

Because you're now on the UI thread, it's possible to modify the contents of the loading status text. Once you've changed the status message, you can begin adding elements to the `ArrayAdapter`. You'll just loop through the size of the vector and add each item to the adapter. How, you may ask, does the list element know what text to insert into the `TextView` that comprises each visual element in the list? Simple, look back to that `toString` method you overrode in your `StationData` class. When building the list, the `ArrayAdapter` calls `toString` on each element in the array and displays that text onscreen.

Selection...

You now have a functioning, selectable list of radio stations! Of course, you don't do anything when an item is selected, so you'll have to do something about that. Thankfully, the `ListView`'s tight integration with the `ListActivity` makes this a breeze. Simply override the protected method:

```
protectedvoid onListItemClick(
    ListView l, View v, int position, long id)
{
    StationData selectedStation =
    stationListVector.elementAt(position);
    MediaPlayer player = new MediaPlayer();
    try
    {
        player.setDataSource(selectedStation.url);
        player.start();
    }
    catch (Exception e)
    {
        Log.e("PlayerException", "SetData");
    }
}
```

I've included the audio code that is, as far as I can tell, correct according to the documentation. Just because the documentation says that it works doesn't, however, mean that it actually will work. In fact, the previous code, which links to a Shoutcast MP3 link, doesn't throw an exception but doesn't play. I can only hope the Android engineers resolve this issue before the application launches.

There's been lively debate and lots of example code running around on the Web. A little work with Google's search engine will unfold the multitude of hacky workarounds.

Caution   Nowhere in this example application have I done any useful error handling. Mostly I'll catch exceptions and print something to a log. Your eventual mobile app will have to be better about errors than I'm currently being, because, trust me, networking on the mobile can be a bit touch-and-go.

The Next Step

The final step in this chapter is to give the `ListView` a little panache. You'll want to add a background to the entire screen. Doing this should look a little familiar, because you've done it before in a previous example (see Code Listing 5-10).

Code Listing 5-10. Linear Layout XML Block Inside `Main.xml`

```
<LinearLayout xmlns:android=
  "http://schemas.android.com/apk/res/android"
    android:orientation="vertical"
    android:layout_width="fill_parent"
    android:layout_height="fill_parent"
    android:background="@drawable/bg"
>
```

`@drawable/bg` refers, of course, to an image inside the `/res/drawable/` directory. You'll also want to adjust the width of the list widget:

```
<ListView android:id="@+id/android:list"
        android:layout_width="fill_parent"
        android:layout_height="fill_parent"
        />
```

This will keep the menu elements from changing size element by element, which, I think you can agree, looks pretty horrendous. Setting a list view layout width or height to `wrap_content` causes it to wrap each menu item individually. Go figure.

Dressing Up the Menu

There is one more major change you can make to the menu that will give you a little more control over rendering it.

Android allows you, when defining the UI elements for the adapter, to specify a large menu item object and then point to a `TextView` inside that you'd like edited. Before, you would point to a single, predefined

TextView. Code Listing 5-11 shows what your new list element layout file will look like.

Code Listing 5-11. The New and Improved `list_element.xml`

```
<?xml version="1.0" encoding="utf-8"?>
<LinearLayout xmlns:android=
    "http://schemas.android.com/apk/res/android"
    android:orientation="vertical"
    android:layout_width="fill_parent"
    android:layout_height="22dip"
    android:background="@drawable/listbg"
>
<TextView android:id="@+id/textElement"
        xmlns:android=
      "http://schemas.android.com/apk/res/android"
        android:layout_width="fill_parent"
        android:layout_height="fill_parent"
        android:textAlign="center"
        />
</LinearLayout>
```

In this code, you've added a linear layout with some specific dimensions. You've also given it the background `listbg.png`. Interestingly enough, Android will rescale your background image to fit the space of the calculated background size. You may wonder, if you've done your homework, why you're using a linear layout instead of just adding a background and dimensions to the previous text view. You're doing this simply for demonstrative reasons. I want you, when you make an application that's much better than mine, to see how complex lists can be put together. Before I wrap up, there's one more line in the code you need to update to make this change. It's within the `initList` method:

```
private void initList()
{
adapter = new ArrayAdapter<StationData>(
  StationPicker.this, R.layout.list_element,
   R.id.textElement);
 . . . . . . . . . . . . . .
```

```
setListAdapter(adapter);
}
```

In the previous Adapter initializer, you specified only the layout element. Now you need to point to a file in the `/res/folder/` that contains the more complicated list element as well as a pointer that tells Android where to place the text pulled from the `toString` function of the `StationData` object.

Now, if you've done everything correctly (or you've cheated and downloaded the sample file), you should see the layout looking like Figure 5-1.

Frankly, thanks to my abysmal graphic designer skills, this version of the UI couldn't be described as pretty. It probably also couldn't be described as good. The point is not to make fun of my poor sense of graphical design, although you're more than welcome to do so. The point is that this example should show you how to make your application look better than my example. Now you can use nearly anything to construct this menu.

Figure 5-1. The dressed-up station list

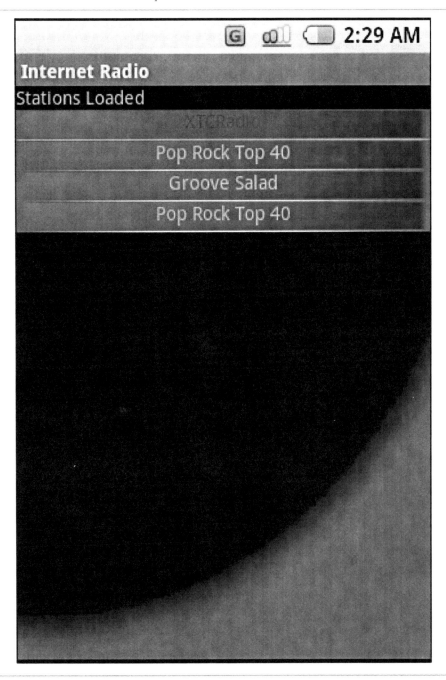

Looking Back

Over the course of this chapter, you've had a chance to let Android stretch its legs a little bit. I covered basic networking, some more in-depth UI layout, and a little XML parsing to boot.

The HTTP layer is straightforward and easy to use at this point, despite being cumbersome and slow (at least on the OS X emulator). Android clearly has the ability to delve into proxies, cookies, socket-level connections, and much more advanced web-fu. You were able to get into downloading data, using XML data, and using a SAX parser to stuff it into a vector. From this `Vector`, you built up a list that, when an item is selected, launched into some theoretical media streamer. Sadly, the media-streaming capabilities don't live up to its documentation, but, over time, this is something that should be remedied.

Chapter 6: Tying on a Bow

It's almost time to stop reading and start writing your Android application. Before I let you go, I'll quickly run through where you went and how you got there.

The Making of an Application

My first task was to cover the basic building blocks of an Android application. I also had to cover creating a new project and the logistics of building and running it. As I discussed, an application consists of a series of activities, intent receivers, services, and content resolvers. I used a splash screen implementation to demonstrate activities, an SMS-triggered prank application to explore intent receivers and services, and finally some simple bookmaking code to get into content resolvers.

Thankfully, Android provides a series of clear and simple building blocks with which to create your application. Activities form the backbone of any Android app, with intents and intent receivers acting as the communication officers. Services and content resolvers cater to very specific needs such as background processes and formatted data transmission. Put all these pieces together, and you're left with a robust system for quickly turning around mobile applications.

Looks Aren't Everything, Except, of Course, When They Are

Once you've developed a working application platform, you can make it look like something users might be interested in actually paying for, or not, as you choose. You can build a UI in Android in two general ways. You can use the built-in widgets or views in combination with view groups to create a tiered hierarchy of UI elements. Or, you can toss these custom-built tools aside and do it yourself using nothing but a canvas and some simple line, circle, and bitmap image-rendering tools. Android provides an

XML layout with which you can build your UI widget hierarchy. Additionally, you can build, manipulate, and tweak these very same views and view groups inside your code.

By using these two methods in combination, you can predesign all your static pieces (preformatted menus, backgrounds, help screens) while adding and manipulating these elements within the code to react to network and dynamic data. Lastly, you can specify canvas areas both in code and in XML where data can be drawn by hand. Although Android's views and view groups can be overcomplicated and difficult to use at first, in some rare cases it mostly leaves us developers with more power and flexibility than any other platform I've known.

To explore this raw opportunity and flexibility, you wrote a simple login/password screen, created a main menu using only raw Java code and `TextView` objects, and finally fiddled with some auditory illusions using the raw canvas.

Location Isn't Too Important, Except When You Need Pizza at 4 a.m.

Once you have the solid foundations of the application logic and the user interface, you can move on to much more interesting and exciting topics. You can explore subjects such as Android's GPS and Google Maps service.

Android gives you multiple ways to access the location of the handset. Although the emulated implementation is rather crude, the documentation suggests that much more is possible with the final running version. To get a taste for these two powerful mobile functions, you made a slightly less powerful location-tracking example. A blue tack would, assuming you got everything right, follow along with the emulator's imaginary tromp through Silicon Valley. The example should, when run on an actual handset, choose a rather more efficient method of position determination and follow the user with that same annoying tack.

Taking Off Android's Leash and Letting It Romp Around the Internet

Last, you took the opportunity to let Android roam the Internet at large. You pulled down a simple XML file, parsed it, pushed its contents into a list, and then failed, thanks to Android's incomplete networking layer, at making Android stream audio over the network. Along the way, you discovered the joys of adapters and list views in both their primitive and somewhat more complex forms.

Overall

Over the course of all these chapters, I've tried to arm you with a general foundation from which to create your own mobile application. It's simply impossible, in the short time we have together, to convey and explain every option available to you, the Android developer. Instead, I've tried to give you a grasp of the fundamentals and the essential building blocks and understanding required to create your next killer application.

Other Sources of Information

As Android gains popularity, I'm sure you'll see more sources of information begin to spring up. There are already several blogs, websites, wikis, forums, and other information resources out there. A few good Google searches should get you on your way. For now, make sure you bookmark the Android online documentation found here:

```
http://code.google.com/android/documentation.html
```

There's also a team building the Android documentation into Javadoc format here:

```
http://www.androidjavadoc.com/
```

You can find more information in Google's "Getting Started Guide" here:

```
http://code.google.com/android/intro/index.html
```

Last, a few more advanced (now that you've mostly covered the basics) topics in the tutorials can further help you on your way. Be sure to check them out here:

```
http://code.google.com/android/intro/tutorial.html
```

Getting Help

Google also provides a few helpful resources for when you get stuck. Here's a link to the Android beginners forum:

```
http://groups.google.com/group/android-beginners
```

Also, as a developer, your main stomping grounds will be over in the more general form area:

```
http://groups.google.com/group/android-developers
```

Be sure to check the other Google groups as well. They can be an invaluable resource.

It's Time to Stop Reading and Start Helping

Seriously, we, as a community of mobile developers, need help. Currently, our achievements include sending picture messages, downloading MP3 ringtones, and browsing a small, walled garden of the Web. We need you, your abilities, your gumption, and your creativity to turn this proverbial bus around. The cracks are beginning to show. Verizon and AT&T are now vying for the title of "Most Open Network." People are hacking the iPhone SDK, and indeed, Apple is making its own official SDK available, as limited and confining as it is.

Geeks are starting to do to the mobile world what they did for the desktop computing one. They're starting to innovate in spite of the blocks put up to prevent them from doing so. Android, in my opinion, represents the highest level of access to a handset second only to Qualcomm's BREW SDK. This is one of the major reasons I agreed to write this book (well, that and I didn't want to learn Objective-C).

Android, if allowed to flourish by OEMs and carriers, represents the potential for a breakthrough we mobile developers have waited for. Please, step up, and take the tools the Open Handset Alliance and Google have given us and make something amazing with it. We're counting on you. Good luck.

Copyright

Printed in the United States
125968LV00004B/63-68/P